THINKING MATTERS

THINKING MATTERS

A Guide to Making Wiser and More Thoughtful Decisions

SELMA WASSERMANN

ROWMAN & LITTLEFIELD
Lanham • Boulder • New York • London

Published by Rowman & Littlefield
An imprint of The Rowman & Littlefield Publishing Group, Inc.
4501 Forbes Boulevard, Suite 200, Lanham, Maryland 20706
www.rowman.com

86-90 Paul Street, London EC2A 4NE, United Kingdom

British Library Cataloguing in Publication Information Available

Library of Congress Cataloging-in-Publication Data

Names: Wassermann, Selma, author.
Title: Thinking matters : a guide to making wiser and more thoughtful decisions / Selma Wassermann.
Description: Lanham, Maryland : Rowman & Littlefield, 2024. | Includes bibliographical references. | Summary: "Thinking Matters offers adults an opportunity to examine what it means to use intelligent habits of mind to make wise, rational, and informed choices and to deal more logically with the problems that impact their lives"—Provided by publisher.
Identifiers: LCCN 2023052164 (print) | LCCN 2023052165 (ebook) | ISBN 9781475873870 (cloth) | ISBN 9781475873887 (paperback) | ISBN 9781475873894 (epub)
Subjects: LCSH: Thought and thinking. | Decision making.
Classification: LCC BF441 .W34 2024 (print) | LCC BF441 (ebook) | DDC 153.4/2—dc23/eng/20231219
LC record available at https://lccn.loc.gov/2023052164
LC ebook record available at https://lccn.loc.gov/2023052165

Contents

ACKNOWLEDGMENTS

It is my family to whom I owe the most appreciation for their continued support, confidence in, and regard for my work as a writer and teacher. My longtime mate and husband Jack, daughter Paula, grandsons Arlo and Simon, and great grandchildren Ruben, Maya, and Kai have each made singular and valued inputs into my life and work, and they all stand at the head of my list. Without Simon, the Wizard of Parksville, and his expert high-tech help with my computer problems, I'd probably still be writing with a pencil and a yellow pad.

Colleagues Larry Cuban, George Ivany, and Bill Cliett have written not only positive but also enthusiastic responses to a request to weigh in on the merits of the proposal for this new book, and I am deeply indebted to them for their support.

And to the memory of my great teacher and mentor, Louis E. Raths, whose original work and theoretical constructs continue to inform my own thinking and writing, my ongoing and heartfelt thanks.

Preface

When my grandmother was a young woman, raising six children at the turn of the last century, she lived in a cold-water tenement with a bathroom in the backyard. Every meal she cooked had to be made from scratch, by hand. There were no electric mixers, no food processors, no refrigerator, and no washing machine.

All the marketing had to be done by walking to the shops and carrying the parcels up the three flights of stairs. A neighborhood grocery carried only the most basic supplies, all of which were locally sourced. Supermarkets were unheard of with their vast array of foods from all over the world. My grandfather worked as a tailor, into the late hours of the night, to provide what he could to keep the family in food and shelter. There were no unions to protect his trade; he had to take what he could get and make the best of it. The two older children were taken out of school at age 12 and sent to work to help support the family. No child labor laws kept them safe and in school.

Sanitation was not high on the list of civic concerns, and garbage and waste littered the streets. Children died of diphtheria, smallpox, scarlet fever, and infantile paralysis. The Spanish flu wiped out 50 million people worldwide because knowledge of how the disease was transmitted was yet to be understood. There were no antidotes, no vaccines, and no penicillin to combat infection. Doctors thought that washing their hands before doing surgery was "effeminate."

Automobiles were few; they were the "toys" of the very rich. If you needed to go across town, you took a trolley. A big trip was taking the newly installed elevated train to go from Brooklyn to Manhattan.

The role of women was to serve men domestically as well as take care of the children in the household. In fact, a married woman's legal existence was incorporated into that of her husband. Women could not vote or hold public office. They could, by virtue of the Married Women's Property Act, passed in New York in 1848, be allowed to keep their own wages if they held jobs.

Hard times?

In contrast, today I live in a high-rise apartment with every conceivable electrical appliance at my fingertips. I can phone to Whole Foods to ask them to deliver my shopping if I choose. The variety and array of foods available come by refrigerated container ships from all over the world. The computer in my study allows me to read the latest news without having to wait for the delivery of the morning paper. My daughter and grandchildren went to schools that are modern and fully equipped and have the best-trained teachers.

A vast selection of recreational activities are at our fingertips; we have the cinema, the theater, the symphony, and the opera, all housed in elegant venues and styles. Streaming allows me to sit at home and watch the latest movies. I can use my cell phone to call anyone so connected anywhere in the world. It also takes photos and videos, and with it, I can download e-books. If I choose, I can leave my Pacific coast residence and arrive in time to have New York pizza for dinner that same evening.

Modern medicine has given us vaccines to combat polio and other infectious diseases. Even the COVID-19 pandemic found scientists working around the clock to find a vaccine that would, at least, reduce the flu symptoms if infected or, better, gave us the resources to combat the infection in the first place.

Compared to the early 20th century, life today, for many of us, is one of comparative ease.

Better times?

And yet there are many now who claim that we, who live in the most highly lauded democracy in the world, are on the verge of a breakdown of that democracy. Problems like the wrangling between political parties, political polarization, social divisions, racial tensions, the wealth gap, and the dangers of climate change have become more acute. There are approximately 600,000 homeless people living on the streets and in shelters in this, the richest country in the world. All of these conditions (and others) are pointed to as "weakening the functioning of democracy in the United States."

A former president made false claims of election fraud that brought a frightening army of rioters to the steps of Congress, making an assault on the very halls of our highest democratic institution. Threatened elected officials fled in fear of their lives. All of this was viewed by millions on their home TV sets as they cringed in horror at what should have been a peaceful transfer of power.

The internet, while giving us immediate access to a world of information, has also become a source of disinformation, intimidation, infiltration, and scamming, leaving a large group of "users" unable and unready to differentiate between what is real and what is fiction—between what facts are supported by data and what are blatant lies. When a president's press secretary talks about "alternate truths" as a reliable source of evidence, whom are we to believe?

The murders of children in schools by lunatics with easy access to guns has become a weekly horror show; the *New York Times* reported that more than 49,000 people were murdered by guns during 2021, citing that there are more guns owned in the United States than there are people.

In our "lives of ease," we are also witness to the rapid erosion of the health of our planet; violent hurricanes, earthquakes, overpowering snowstorms, devastating wildfires, torrential rains, excessive heat, and the despoiling of Earth have raised the alarm about what our future holds if we continue, as we have been doing, to ruin the lands we live on.

The worst of times?

There is no question that we now live in turbulent times. It is difficult for even adults to make sense of what they see and hear all around them. Not only are we being bombarded by massive amounts of information from multimedia sources, but the pace of information flow is faster than ever. "Spin" has become elevated to a new art form; the distortion and manipulation of data make it increasingly difficult even for adults to discern disinformation from truth.

Many citizens, facing these enormous problems and issues, lacking the resources to deal with them, respond with anger, violence, and attacks on presumed enemies they hold responsible for their personal difficulties. When people are feeling so threatened and so unable to cope, it is understandable they would resort to violence. Frustration does, in fact, breed aggression.

But the resources to deal with the problems in a free society are attainable. They lie in our ability to take time to reflect, to observe, to study, to inquire, and to make intelligent meaning of what is happening all around us. They lie in our ability to make informed decisions based on data analysis and to acquire the more sophisticated problem-solving skills that give us the resources and the power to tackle the problems that lie ahead. Absent these more intelligent habits of mind, our democracy might, indeed, be in peril.

INTRODUCTION

A mind is a terrible thing to waste.

When it comes to the issue of the development of intelligent habits of mind, there's good news and bad news. The good news is that such higher-level mental skills, like studying and learning any sophisticated set of skills, can be improved with practice—as we would do when learning a foreign language, a concerto, calculus, and coding.

The bad news is that such skills don't come spontaneously. We are not born with them. They do not come as a by-product of lesson learning. One can study the names and dates of historical events, learn the formulas of chemical compounds, and memorize correct spelling. But while these may be worthwhile endeavors, they do not serve higher-order mental development. One cannot expect listening to Glenn Gould play the *Bach Goldberg Variations* to translate to one's own competence on the keyboard. To learn to play the *Goldberg Variations*, there's no getting around sitting down at the piano and practicing.

Alas, there's more bad news. Nearly 100 years ago, Aldous Huxley, in his classic novel *Brave New World*, wrote about a future utopian society in which monogamy, family, and privacy have all been outlawed to produce a society without "issues." People who have problems with this utopia are offered a drug called "soma," which numbs any discomfort, from anxiety to stress to general unease. The drug is handed out like M&M's to adults and children from a small dispenser that is carried around in a pocket.

In our contemporary culture, we have our own forms of soma. Social media give us solace when we are distressed, an outlet for our anger, companionship when we are lonely. Tablets and mobile phones take our minds off what is happening under our noses, a form of escapism that has become endemic. The "metaverse" of unlimited entertainment has distracted us and so dazed us by their fictions that we are in danger of losing our sense of what is real (Garber 2023). Postman's (1985) caution about our need to "amuse ourselves to death" is more real today than when he wrote in 1985.

And now, with ChatGPT, we don't have to do our own thinking anymore. Artificial intelligence (AI) does it for us.

The evidence suggests that we do live in perilous times for the development of intelligent habits of mind. Several states in the United States have, with legislation, banned certain topics of discussion from elementary, secondary, and university classrooms so that students may not learn about certain critical issues in history. Slavery and its impact on the lives of those enslaved, endemic racism, African American history, inequality, gender preferences, and sex education are all off-limits in these states.

"Parents, activists, school board officials, and lawmakers are challenging books and topics at a pace not seen in decades" (*New York Times*, September 24, 2022). This may mean that teachers who believe their roles to be the opening of students' minds to the examination of critical issues may lose their jobs.

In some universities, it has become dangerous for a lecturer to offer ideas that seem discrepant with the views of certain student groups. Freedom of speech, a prized value of a republic, is jeopardized by speaking about issues that are thought to be not "politically correct." "Cancel culture is quite real in the U.S. and its effects have been toxic to debate, and in many cases, to institutional decision making" (Chotiner 2020).

How far have we come from the time when Socrates, in 339 B.C., was made to drink hemlock for corrupting the youth of Athens with his "progressive ideas"? How far have we come from the time when heretics, those espousing against organized religious dogma, were burned at the stake? How far have we come from the time of the Scopes trial, when it was illegal for teachers to teach about human evolution in any state-funded school?

There is no question that this book, on how to improve our intelligent habits of mind, comes at a propitious time. Yes, we do live in turbulent times. Yes, there are initiatives afoot in many states that would put a halt to opening children's minds about topics that those in power would choose to muzzle. Yes, there are those in positions of power who wish to manipulate thinking to serve their own political ends. Yes, we are deluged with misinformation from certain media outlets that confuse and befuddle us about what is true and whom to believe.

How do we respond? How are we to interpret the data and make sense of what we see and hear? We have options. We can go to ChatGPT and other AI programs to tell us what to do, what to think, and how—our own form of soma. Or we can develop those higher-order mental faculties that give us the means and the ability and the power to think for ourselves, to make rational decisions based on evidence.

So this book is a cri de coeur for us to take charge of our lives and be in charge of them, not to give power to others to tell us what and how to think but to make our own decisions, to figure out the best ways for ourselves, and to feel confident in how our actions might make a positive difference to our lives. It is to those ends that the materials in this book are offered.

How the Book Is Organized

Chapters 1 and 2 provide a discussion of the nature of thinking processes and the reasons that make higher-order thinking an imperative for a people in a democratic society. Chapter 3 describes many of the mental traps that are impediments to rational reasoning. Chapters 4 to 7 provide an organized and systematic approach to the improvement of one's higher-order intellectual functioning.

It is a cliché to remind readers that there is "no free lunch." Implicit in choosing these materials for self-development is the caveat, "What's important to me?" One has to believe, truly believe, that the possession of improved habits of thinking will make a critical difference in one's life, that such skills will make one's life more satisfying, and that such skills will add immeasurably to one's sense of personal power. For surely there is more satisfaction in being able to figure out, for oneself, what to do, how to do it, and why than it is to seek answers and solve problems with the aid of ChatGPT.

These are the questions to consider as you approach the materials within. For those of you embarking on that course of action, I offer the comments of Eddie M., age 12, who, when asked how he felt about facing the problems, pressures, and rigorous programs of high school after engaging in a course of study dedicated to "teaching for thinking" in grade 6, said with full confidence, "We are such independent thinkers, we can handle any new problem."

CHAPTER 1

What Is Thinking?

IF A CHIMP, CONFINED TO A CAGE, USES A LONG STICK TO REACH OUT and grasp a bunch of bananas, is it thinking?

When Picasso created *Guernica*, was he thinking?

When T. S. Eliot wrote *The Wasteland*, was he thinking?

When you face an opponent in a chess match, are your thinking?

When a four-year-old builds a tower with Kiva blocks, is she thinking?

When Sally says she loved the film, is she thinking?

When you fill out your income tax forms, are you thinking?

Is dreaming a form of thinking? Is painting? Is driving a car? Is answering e-mails?

Was the development of a vaccine to combat COVID-19 a form of thinking?

Is remembering the words of an old song thinking?

* * *

What is thinking? This might seem a frivolous question since everybody has some acquaintance with the term and with the experience. We all think from time to time. Even if we are not scientists, artists, inventors, or poets, we have, at least, put ourselves to a task that required some mental challenge. Most of us know very well how some kinds of thinking make sense, are rational, follow an argument with logic, while others seem illogical and make no sense.

Those who have, in the distant past, given descriptions of what a person does when they are thinking were the philosophers. It is only more recently that behavioral psychologists have attempted to find out what happens when we think and what conditions influence our thinking-related behaviors. Alas, in neither philosophy nor psychology have the results been truly successful. But, at the least, they have shown that "thinking" is a much more complicated business than we might have imagined.

What we have learned is that there are many forms of thinking—some more creative and imaginative, some more fantastic, some involving recall and remembering, and others that require more complex mental functioning, called "critical," "rational," or "logical." From all of these reports, what can be determined is that some forms of thinking lead to more reasoned and more reasonable behaviors and outcomes, while other forms may lead one down the proverbial garden path. Thompson ([1959] 1963) might have been the first psychologist to identify the relationship between thinking and behavior: "If we want to study the thinking of an individual, we need to take note of everything he does."

In other words, absent of a precise definition of what happens in the mind when "thinking" occurs, we can make careful observations of how a person behaves, how they interact with their environment, how they respond to certain stimuli, how they act in different situations calling for making considered judgments, and, not the least, what statements are coming out of their mouths.

It was the work of Louis E. Raths and colleagues (1966, 1986) that led to more informed awareness of the relationship between thinking and behavior and the various mental processes that involved more complex and higher-level thought. Based on a substantive amount of research,

Raths was able to conclude that thinking skill development, on higher cognitive levels, required the intelligent exercising of specific types of mental activities. These include comparing, observing, hypothesizing, classifying, collecting and organizing data, problem solving, identifying assumptions, interpreting data, making decisions, summarizing, evaluating, imagining, and creating.

Raths also suggested that various forms of maladaptive behaviors gave evidence of inadequate experiences with higher-order thinking—that children and adults who have not become habituated to the use of higher mental processes have become "chronic non-thinkers." Such behaviors that reflect such shortcomings in the extreme are seen in the following:

Impulsiveness: Jumping to conclusions in the absence of examination of data; rushing to action without consideration of alternatives; needing to act before deliberation; actions directed by whim or caprice.

Overdependency: Needing constant help from others in choosing or acting; unable to work out solutions for themselves.

Extreme dogmatism: Being unyielding about their own opinions; unable to consider alternative points of view; reluctant to acknowledge that there are alternatives; they "know what they know" and are disinclined to consider conflicting data; wedded to conspiracy theories and irrational beliefs.

Missing the meaning: Unable to understand the important meanings in speech or in what is read or heard; unable to distill accurate information from an experience; unable to discriminate the key points of what is read or heard.

Lack of confidence: Lacking belief in their own ideas as having merit; feeling unsafe in offering their own ideas to public scrutiny.

Extreme rigidity: Being stuck "in a rut" with respect to attempting anything new; feeling safer in sticking to old and familiar routines; shying away from new ideas, new strategies.

Means–ends confusion: Using strategies and techniques to solve a problem that are inconsistent or inappropriate to the goals; goals may be unrealistic or impractical; there is no relationship between what they hope to accomplish and the techniques used to attain those goals.

"Anti-think": Failing to value thinking as a means to achieve goals; is action oriented rather than "thoughtful;" sees "thinking" as a waste of time; detests discussions, research, independent work; believes "answers" are to be found on the internet or in the TV programs that affirm ideas that are consistent with their own views.

* * *

These thinking-related behaviors are not definitions of what "higher-order thinking" constitutes; instead, they provide some indicators of what is seen in a person's behavior that suggests an absence of rationality, a "missing" cerebral gene, or a discrepancy between what is logical and what is surreal or false or purely irrational. The categories are not writ in stone; rather, they are crude descriptions, signs of what to look for in the absence of rational thought. They might not answer the question of "what is thinking?," but they surely provide some clues, some starting points in the quest to comprehend the nature of and the absence of rational behavior.

CHAPTER 2

Why Think?

A person cannot be both stupid and free.

For thousands of years, the primary aim of humankind was to survive, and most of early human's thinking served this end. With "progress," there came a time when humans could plan not only to live but also to live better. Using those early intellectual skills, they learned to house themselves more comfortably, to make fire, to hunt more profitably, to find food that would be more satisfying, and to care more adequately for their young.

As humans became more social, they created social problems. They laid out territorial claims and made wars with other tribes and groups who would attempt to invade their territory. They learned that group work was more productive than working alone. They learned better ways to keep warm, to feed themselves, to care for their young. And in using those new methods, they became stronger and lived longer. These were some of the problems that challenged the thinking of early humans.

There was—and continues to be—no end to the problems that confront humankind. These problems have become more urgent today than ever before, so this is one reason for the need to develop those higher-order mental processes.

There are probably very few among us who would doubt the importance of intelligent reasoning. With our abilities to think rationally come the concomitant skills to be more self-directing, more considerate, and more thoughtful. With intelligent reasoning, we become less rash, less hasty, less intemperate in our judgments, and less prone to conspiracy theories and irrational beliefs.

Our ability to reason, to be rational, gives us the means to use those skills to see through propaganda, through distortion, and through the imparting of disinformation that attempts to persuade us that up is down, that lies are truth, that there are simplistic answers to complex problems, and that a self-aggrandizing and duplicitous leader will lead us out of the morass of our difficulties to greener pastures. Our intelligence gives us the tools to come up with new ideas and new inventions; it allows us to dream dreams of what is possible and how we can achieve our goals.

Why is this important? Because it is not an exaggeration to claim that our survival depends on it, because we realize we can't be both incompetent and free. The republic that we have built demands intelligence; a society that cannot or will not think about how to deal with its problems will not remain free and independent.

All of the social institutions of a republic play an important role in the shaping of that society. In every hour of every day, we are, through the decisions we make, contributing toward the development of that society. The more we act rationally, thoughtfully, and with care, the better our chances of surviving to the next century—perhaps not us ourselves but our children and grandchildren. Their very future may depend on our rational actions and on how we deal with the problems facing us right now.

This is the universal view, but there are more personal payoffs. It may not be obvious but there is a one-to-one relationship between a person's ability to use intelligent habits of mind and their feelings of personal power. There is an innate sense of "can-do" that is intensely satisfying when we can figure things out on our own, when we have solved a difficult problem, or when we have broken new ground. "Please, Mom, I'd rather do it myself" is the urgent demand of a young child who knows that such personal accomplishment feeds the ego. If Mother does it for them, it is a denial of that source of personal power.

This sense of "power-to" is directly related to one's intellectual functioning. It is also related to ego strength, to self-confidence, and to heightened personal autonomy. Persons with a well-developed sense of power-to are adults who are able to be "in charge" of their lives. Rogers (1961) has referred to these adults as fully functioning. We have seen them in our professional and social circles, among our friends, and in the marketplace of life, and we admire them. There is a positive spirit about them. In tough situations, they are able to take charge. Their actions reveal thoughtful and well-reasoned planning.

When faced with a problem requiring some innovative procedures, they do not shirk; rather, they embrace the problem with positive energy. We trust them to find solutions. Their confidence in themselves fills us with confidence in them. A very good example of such a person is Richard Feynman. That he took the Nobel Prize in physics is only one indication of his extraordinary can-do spirit. What is even more extraordinary is that he lived with an unshakable belief in his own capability to *do*. This allowed him to take on tasks far outside of his original area of expertise. "Safecracking," painting, and learning the bongo drum were some of his other skills requiring quite diverse talents. And he succeeded in doing them with remarkable ease.

When Feynman was faced with a problem that required an immediate solution and for which he had no previous experience, he invariably began with a positive attitude about his potential for finding a solution. And inevitably, he found one (Feynman 1985).

But what of those among us who have not had a chance to develop that sense of power-to? What kinds of behaviors serve them, and why are those behaviors so counterproductive?

There are a great many words and phrases to describe immature behavior. Many of them are associated with thinking or, more properly, with its neglect. We may say of a person that they are like children, forever dependent on adults to help them solve problems. We may say that a person is very impulsive and doesn't take time to think, leaping to conclusions that are not supported by data. We may say that some people are so wedded to their own beliefs that they are unable to entertain or to consider a different point of view.

There is no question that such behaviors are maladaptive; they put people at a disadvantage in the sense that they are not playing with a full deck. They are absent of those critical faculties that enhance lives—those tools that include self-initiative, resourcefulness, creativity, and a high degree of problem-solving skills—imperative not only for those who live in a free society but also so that they can live more satisfying and purposeful lives.

Why is thinking important? Ever since humans descended from trees, they have been using logic to avoid extinction. Sometimes logic has failed them dismally, but success has been more frequent than failure; otherwise, we should not be here to write about it. If humans had not been successful in using their higher-order mental faculties, they would have perished.

CHAPTER 3

Traps to Logical Thinking

Dangerous Grades and Curves the Next 66 Miles

ALTHOUGH MANY OF US WOULD LIKE TO BELIEVE IN OUR CONSUMMATE ability to be logical in the face of decision making, it is also true that there are mental traps that get in the way of rationality, certain "hot-button" topics that impede our ability to act with reason.

Hot-button issues are likely to vary in different social settings, but what is clear is that when emotionality is high, reason and reasonable argument disintegrate. For example, in some social settings, talking about politics seems to generate more heat than light. It is much harder to make a rational decision when angry, sad, hurt, or fearful; it is much harder to make a rational decision when one's ego needs overrule our logic.

Stuart Chase (1956), in his classic book *Guides to Straight Thinking*, identified a dozen "logical fallacies" that stand as impediments to rational thought. Their use in a discussion, argument, or debate shifts the dialogue away from factual information to the gray area of muddled thinking. When these fallacies are used to support an argument, it should immediately raise the alarm that the speaker is treading on thin ice.

Some of these and other "mind traps" are described here to illustrate the ways reason slips from us in conversation; on the surface, they may sound reasonable, but with more careful scrutiny, they fail to meet even the most modest standards of rationality.

MIND TRAPS

Mind traps are often defense mechanisms. We use them to protect our egos, to alleviate anxiety, or to fulfill some basic needs. When our anxieties are overwhelming, we may resort to these mind-trap devices to protect ourselves or to protect someone we care about. They may not be under our conscious control, but they do "cloud our minds" and prevent us from seeing clearly, from being unable to differentiate between truth and wishful thinking.

Mind traps like those discussed in this chapter are impediments to rational thinking. In some people, they persist and become part of that person's ways of communicating. Falling into mind traps as a way of dealing with larger life issues or decisions makes us vulnerable; that kind of thinking influences our lives in ways that are not only counterproductive but also dangerous.

Rationalizations

We rationalize to protect our egos, to bolster our self-concepts, and to reduce feelings of stress. It's a very common way of defending ourselves against an unpleasant reality:

> "Oh, Shelly got the promotion instead of me. But you know what? I really didn't want all that responsibility."

> "I know I shouldn't have eaten that second donut. But I didn't want it to go to waste."

> "I got a C in physics. That's because the teacher is prejudiced against women in science."

Rationalizations may be reassuring, but they are also self-serving. They are insidious because people come to believe their own excuses. Although at first a rationalization may sound like it makes sense, the deeper truth is that, on rigorous examination, it fails the logic test.

Emotional Bias

High emotional states play havoc with good judgments, decisions, and behaviors. They influence our reasoning processes and the accuracy of our beliefs. When our emotions are running high, our judgments become more clouded. High anxiety, distress, fear, sadness, and shame all contribute to overwhelming emotionality. In any of these high emotional states, the decisions that we make are less dependable; they come more from the need to relieve the anxiety than from reason.

It was emotional bias that contributed to the great patriotic fervor that uplifted the spirits of British troops as they marched to the trenches in 1914 at the beginning of World War I. That high emotionality, stirred up by slogans and the unrealistic expectations of a wartime adventure, was more than sufficient incentive to lead men to sign up to take the king's shilling—before reality stepped in to reveal the obscenity of the slaughter of life in the trenches. No soldier who lived through the reality of that trench warfare maintained any illusion of that patriotic fervor.

One of the most potent arenas in which emotional bias occurs is in the area of politics. Historically famous hot buttons in politics have been taxes, immigration, abortion, the economy, the debt ceiling, guns, crime, climate crisis, AI, and racism—to mention a few. Politicians are well versed in drumming up emotional heat to gain political advantage and the votes of those who are easily persuaded by heated emotional arguments.

Dogmatism

To be dogmatic is to be certain when suspended judgment is called for. A dogmatic argument is one in which a person's belief system is unyielding in the face of further consideration. So strong is their personal conviction that they are blinded to conflicting data. Dogmatic people are rigid about what they think; their arguments reveal a lack of appreciation that there are other, more reliable data to consider. In other words, "Don't confuse me with the data. My mind is made up!"

Those who are dogmatic in their assertions may use "confirmation bias" to search for supporting evidence to affirm their beliefs. Not only does this mental trap prevent the consideration of data that contradict their strongly held beliefs, but it also reveals a closed-minded and highly defended persona. Self-awareness is not their strong suit.

One danger of such rigidity in thinking is that these dogmatic thinkers tend to identify with certain pseudo-authorities whom they believe they can trust and whose espoused views tend to confirm and support their beliefs. In that way, they become vulnerable to empty, persuasive messages, such as commercials, slogans, and cries of alarm from self-appointed authorities. According to Kahneman (2011), "Without putting into operation the intelligent habits of mind that come from System 2 thinking, people will believe almost anything."

More often than not, dogmatic mind traps are the breeding grounds for racism, for ethnic prejudice, for social bigotry, and for a litany of irrational beliefs.

Impulsiveness

The person who is impulsive leaps to conclusions without having considered the data. There is an absence of reflection before action; action seems more important than thinking about the best way or about alternatives to pursue. Impulsive thinkers are motivated more by needing to act than by the need to consider the best plan, the most appropriate course, and the most desirable way. Almost never do they consider the consequences of their actions. Their preferred mode of behavior is action rather than thoughtful deliberation.

"I don't understand why we need more discussion. Let's just do it!"

Means–Ends Inconsistencies

At the root of such a mind trap is a person's lack of consideration of how best to achieve one's goals. The route taken, not having been carefully thought out, is either incompatible with or inappropriate to the goal. Consequently, the results of their efforts are doomed. Such inability to think rationally about an appropriate course of action is very frequently frustrating to themselves.

Such mind traps often lie at the root of plans that have been put into effect and that subsequently fail because they are inconsistent with the actions taken. For example, civic leaders put a plan into operation to provide shelter for the homeless. However, the numbers of homeless people needing shelter far overwhelmed the resources, leaving both the homeless and planners frustrated and angry. In another example, the principal of an elementary school "punished" two boys who were accused of bullying by giving them a week's holiday from school (suspension).

Means–end mind traps are perhaps another form of impulsiveness, a need to reach a goal before the alternatives have been examined and provided for. But they are also another form of the way in which logical thinking about the best means to accomplish desired ends fails.

Anti-Intellectual

This mind trap is especially dangerous since such people seem to have put the idea of intelligent thinking on the scale of least desirable traits. Hofstadter (1963) described such people as being "resentful of the life of the mind, and of those considered to represent it; a disposition to minimize the value of that life." Anti-intellectuals view intellectuals as "pretentious, conceited and snobbish, and very likely immoral, dangerous and subversive" (Hofstadter 1963). They are wedded to the idea that plain common sense is an altogether adequate substitute for, if not actually much superior to, formal knowledge and expertise.

Imagine putting a negative value on intelligence. Imagine prizing ignorance over reason. Can a person be stupid and free?

Statistics Prove

In providing an argument in which statistics are offered to prove a point, it is best to remember the old saw: there are lies, damn lies, and statistics. In fact, statistics prove nothing. Statistical fallacies are common tricks that data can play on a person and that lead to mistakes in data interpretation and analysis. While it has been said that "numbers don't lie," it is more true that numbers can be manipulated to lie all the time.

One glaring example of how statistics were used to shape thinking is found in the records of Purdue Pharma, whose then new product OxyContin was advertised as a safe, nonaddictive opioid that was highly effective for pain relief. In promoting this false statement, they used a numerical graph showing that the drug was nonaddictive. The data on the graph showing that OxyContin was beneficial was manipulated to hide the fact that the positive results were false.

It was this misleading graph that resulted in Food and Drug Administration approval that initiated one of the biggest health crises in the United States. The company was forced to pay a fine of $600 million for its criminal actions.

During the infamous McCarthy hearings about the "red scare"—that reckless senator who is now considered a symbol of irrationality and irresponsibility—claimed that there were 205 communists holding government offices in the United States. While his number caused considerable alarm, his report turned out to be completely without merit.

What lesson is learned? Be wary of statistical and other numerical claims that are supposed to reveal "truths."

Unwarranted Assumptions

On the one hand, making assumptions helps us to wade through a lot of information and draw some conclusions. On the other hand, making unwarranted assumptions may cause us to infer data that are wrong or absent, thereby putting us in positions of making decisions that have negative or unintended consequences.

The internet is a minefield of information that we assume to be true. Advertisements on TV or in newspapers are also larded with information intended to persuade us that certain products are more healthful and safer and will make our lives easier and happier. A well-known movie personality advertises that the medicine he takes makes him feel more energetic. A medical clinic in Philadelphia advertises that it can cure cancers that other hospitals cannot cure.

It's not that assumptions themselves are bad. We make all kinds of assumptions each day as we go about living our lives. What is important is the ability to recognize that assumptions are not facts. Because when we offer them as facts or rely on them as factual, we may be headed for trouble.

One of the ways in which unwarranted assumptions get us into trouble is with the kind of attributions we make about others based on their appearance, their skin color, their ethnic backgrounds, the neighborhoods in which they live, their sexual orientation, the kinds of foods they eat, their manner of speech, and other surface attributes. Drawing conclusions about others based on attributions about them is not only faulty but also the underpinnings of prejudicial thinking.

Differentiating assumptions from facts is the key to more intelligent thinking and more rational decision making.

Bogus Authorities

There is the tendency for people, in some arguments, to rely on a "nameless" or an assumed authority to back up some claim. For example, "they" say the Russians are losing the war in Ukraine, "they" say that Biden is too old to finish a second term, "they" say that a flying saucer was spotted in Utah, or "they" say that too much oatmeal is bad for your health. Or, "Tucker Carlson said that the election was rigged."

Such examples of mind traps rely on some "supposed" authority to give credence to one's views. This nameless or assumed person offers about as little support for the truth as one is likely to get.

A dependence on anonymous, unknown, and assumed authorities for verification of truth is a fool's errand. It is an appeal *not* to think but rather to accept because "they" said it was so.

Preferential Blindness

It is probably a given that each of us has, within our own intellectual makeup, a belief that we hold so strong that all discussion and argument are colored by it. Often that preferential blindness is rare and selective. In some cases, it is harmless. For example, we may be blind to the faults of our children, seeing them with rose-colored glasses as never being wrong, as never doing wrong, and as being perfect in every way. We may elevate their skills beyond their actual abilities. We may attribute higher intelligence to them than their actual performance allows.

In G. M. Ford's book *No Man's Land*, he describes a mother whose son has committed two murders: "I will never give up on my son. Never will. As long as both of us live. I'll always be his mother, and I'll always be on his side. Doesn't matter what he has done. I know it wasn't his fault and that someone else was to blame. That's part of being a mother."

Can we be forgiven for those excesses since they are, after all, our children?

Where we are treading on more dangerous ground is when we are blind to a person's talents based on the color of their skin or on their ethnicity. We are on more dangerous ground when we are blind to a person's talents based on their social class. We are on more dangerous ground when we play favorites due to blind prejudice. The dangerous symptom of preferential blindness is deeply held prejudice—for or against. That preferential blindness colors our thinking and shifts us away from rationality to illusion.

Label Bias

Labeling is abusive, derogatory, and insulting. It is seen in the schoolyard by bullies, who use certain labels to mock and ostracize other children. "He's a retard." "She's a spaz." It is heard in social situations when certain "others" who don't belong to the dominant group are given derogatory labels: "She's a social climber." "He's a loser." It is heard in political arguments to downgrade certain candidates: "He's a perv." "He's a low-rent guy."

Not all labels are negative; some elevate the "other" in undeserved ways. But whatever the roots of the labeling, the evidence is clear that they come not from truth or fact but from the narrow thinking of deeply held prejudices. In some instances, the labels about others are used to elevate ourselves over and above those labeled; they are empty and specious ways to serve our egos and have nothing to do with reality.

While it is true that "political correctness" has, to some extent, made us more cautious about using derogatory labels, they nevertheless continue to be used. Negative labeling about others not only impacts their well-being but also points to our own prejudices and fears about our own status. They are facile and immature attributions that are, at their very roots, hateful rhetoric rather than evidence of intelligence.

Sweeping Generalizations

According to Chase (1956), many of us, including the most intelligent, are often falling into the mental trap of making sweeping generalizations that are the "most seductive and potentially the most dangerous of all the mental traps." A person drives through a town and sees a few stores shuttered and says, "This town is on the verge of collapse; nothing but closed shops." A car passes you on the road, and you claim, "The drivers in this town are just plain nuts."

"Did you know that redheads get angry more easily?"

"The tallest basketball players are the best."

"Mexicans are criminals, drug dealers, rapists," according to Donald Trump.

When we cite a generalization to encompass everyone or everything based on a single example, it is a sign of a mental trap that is built on deeply held prejudice. A single case or two leads to an all-encompassing simplification—about redheads, about basketball players, about drivers, or about towns and cities. It quickly can extend to people of color, to immigrants, and to people of other religions. It is common currency in people who use slogans, signs, and labels as universals.

Sweeping generalizations are not truths; they are sloppy ways in which our deeply held prejudices are revealed. They lead us down the garden path of simple judgments when thoughtful consideration is more appropriate. To be aware of them and how we use them gives us insight into what we believe, what we think, and how we think.

Rush to Judgment

Perhaps the internet is to blame for our obsessive/compulsive inclination to comment judgmentally on virtually everything that comes our way. All you need to do it click "like"—no matter the event, person, situation, or issue—to indicate that you have made a judgment about it. No thinking required. Just a click. The more one clicks, the more one becomes habituated to rushing to judgment before the many and various elements of the situation have been considered.

In some instances, the result is nonsignificant. What does it matter if a person "likes" a photo of a cute kitten or puppy, a view of the Alps, or an adorable grandchild? Where it does matter—and it matters a great deal—is when the issue, photo, situation, or person is judged based on surface or ill-considered factors. Where it does matter is when we become habituated to making judgments without thought, without consideration, and without weighing the elements on which that judgment is made and their consequences.

It's not only that such rush to judgment is frivolous; it may be perilous in matters of life or death, as in the case of a police officer rushing to judgment about a person of color's guilt, as in the case of assigning blame to a child for an infraction of the rules, as in the case of attributing evil intentions to migrants, or as in the case of judging a person on the basis of clothes, hair, skin color, ethnic background, or social class.

Such a rush to judgment betrays not only a lack of thoughtful consideration but also a reliance on surface factors that arise from one's personal prejudices. It is not only wrongheaded; it is reckless, biased, and destructive.

HERE'S THE THING

The mind traps cited here are not the only impediments to rationality; as can be noted, there are overlaps in the categories as well. They should not be accepted as the final words about the various ways in which critical reasoning is hampered by some mental jiujitsu that, on the surface, may sound reasonable but on further examination fails the logic test. The important issue, in discussion, debate, and argument, is to ask for supporting evidence and to ascertain, as far as possible, the validity of that evidence.

There is some evidence to support the case that there are people whose persistent and general behavior operates largely in the domain of irrationality. They are not "mentally ill." They have rather become habituated to using mind-trap devices to sustain belief in their misguided ideas. In actual fact, they may never have had the opportunity to exercise and develop those intelligent habits of mind that we associate with wisdom.

There are also people who, in certain situations, use irrational statements to achieve a self-serving goal or some political capital. In other words, they are not habitual anti-intellectuals, nor are they habitual rationalizers. They use such arguments to make a specific case, to persuade others of their views, or to be seen as knowledgeable when they are, in fact, ill-informed. These are the ways and means of the demagogue.

Whether such behavior exists in the extreme or in isolated incidents, the results are the same; discussions and conversations that are loaded with irrational statements do not edify, nor do they illuminate. They muddy the waters and wreak havoc with truth.

As the obsessive-compulsive detective portrayed in the old TV series *Monk* would say, "Here's the thing."

It is highly unlikely that people whose behaviors reveal statements loaded with mind traps—in other words, whose behaviors are irrational in the extreme—would admit to or recognize the fallacies of their statements. Owning up to one's own irrational reasoning skills is a rare commodity among the human species. Highly defended people, who have an ego-invested interest in believing they are right, will least likely be persuaded to "take another look." Alas, there is no argument to be made to persuade people in this group to accept their fallacies in rational thinking. And they may be a lost cause.

On the other hand, there are those who acknowledge and admit that their reasoning abilities may need some work. Among this group are those who are more "open minded" and who are less defensive and less vulnerable to external pressures to accept statements without consideration of accuracy, consistency with other data, and rationality.

It has been noted that there are, in fact, behavioral indications of such open-minded, less defended people. For example, they show tolerance for the ideas and opinions of others and do not believe that their ideas alone are the right ones. They show a tolerance for contrary data in spite of the fact that they may have strong ideas of their own. They have a high tolerance for uncertainty and can live comfortably in the land of uncertainty; uncertainty does not unsettle them.

They are cautious about drawing conclusions where there are insufficient data to support them, and their conclusions are clearly supported by what is known. They embrace thinking as a means of solving problems. Rather than being anti-intellectual, they put a value on thinking as a way to inform their decisions. They are open to self-evaluation and non-defensive in that process.

There are also other behavioral indicators of this group with respect to the nature of their mental functioning. They are able to gather and organize data intelligently and in a way that makes sense. They can give examples to support their ideas. The hypotheses they suggest are reasonable and an appropriate means of addressing a problem. Their hypotheses make sense and represent intelligent explanations of how to go about finding solutions to problems. They are able to make intelligent interpretations of data; they are able to read, listen to, observe information, and draw intelligent meanings from what they have heard, read, or seen. The interpretations they make are based on the data. They do not distort the data to support their own ideas.

They are able to see the differences between opinion and fact and between assumption and fact. They make evaluative judgments that are based on appropriate criteria. And, finally, they are able to make thoughtful, intelligent choices with respect to problems, ethical issues, and moral dilemmas (Wassermann 2009).

It is for those who are seeking more ways to improve such thinking-related skills and intellectual functioning that the following chapters are offered.

CHAPTER 4

Sharpening Your Thinking Skills

Introduction

IT IS PROBABLY NO NEWS THAT THE MENTAL OPERATIONS INCLUDED IN higher-order thinking are, like other, more advanced and sophisticated skills, amenable to improvement. For example, under certain conditions, a person can learn the techniques and strategies involved in downhill skiing, in mastering the art of haute cuisine, in brain surgery, in computer coding, or in fencing. Under certain conditions, a person can learn the techniques and strategies involved in improving their more intelligent habits of mind.

Several researchers have added to our understanding of how these higher-order skills can be further developed (e.g., Costa 1985; Paul and Elder 2002; Pogrow 2005; Segal, Chipman, and Glaser 1985; Sternberg 2007). But as we extract from these suggestions, what is clear is that some mental activities require that we "do something more" with information—something more than merely absorbing it from a page and recalling the facts. This "more" involves more sophisticated and intelligent examination of that information; that analysis, in turn, leads to increased understanding of the important issues.

The early work of Louis Raths and colleagues (1966, 1986) provided us with a group of "tools"—strategies that can be used to enhance and improve our thinking skills. Much research in the area of thinking skills development has been carried out in the past 50 years that lend support to Raths's theory—that thinking skills, like other skill sets, can be developed and advanced. These "mental operations" are the basis for the materials in the next section—a comprehensive program of thinking skills development for personal and professional advancement of one's intelligent habits of mind. These operations include the following:

- Comparing
- Observing
- Interpreting data
- Summarizing
- Classifying
- Making decisions
- Suggesting hypotheses
- Creating and inventing
- Evaluating and assessing
- Designing projects and investigations
- Identifying assumptions
- Problem solving

* * *

There are some final comments to be raised before beginning one's work. First, such an undertaking cannot be done half-heartedly. Improvements in one's thinking skills, like learning other sophisticated skills, need thoughtful systematic attention. Second, the work done must be enduring; to expect positive results in a week or a month is folly. And, finally, only if one considers such a program of self-improvement to be of value will they commit themselves to it wholeheartedly.

CHAPTER 5

Sharpening Your Thinking Skills

Gathering Knowledge and Promoting Understanding

IT WILL BE IMMEDIATELY OBVIOUS, FROM EVEN A CURSORY GLANCE AT the activities included in the following pages, that all of the tasks depart from the right-answer orientation of most other textbook exercises. The activities, instead, are "open ended" and allow for a wide variety of responses. It is the quality of thinking that shapes the responses and the in-depth exploration of the material that is important. Right answers are not sought; on the contrary, right answers are more likely to constrain thinking rather than extend it.

This is not to say that right answers are wrong in other contexts. It is rather to say that it is not the orientation of activities that are designed to engage higher-order thought.

The activities are arranged in three groups. The first, in this chapter, includes the mental operations of promoting understanding through comparing, observing, classifying, identifying assumptions, suggesting hypotheses, summarizing, and interpreting data. Chapter 6 includes a second group: applying what is known to practice. The activities in this group include designing projects and investigations, applying principles to new situations, and applying what is known to decision making. Chapter 7 asks for reflections on one's work that includes evaluating and assessing.

All the activities include specific instructions so that the work to be done is clear. For each mental operation, there are three or four tasks, beginning with less complex and advancing to more complex. Each activity has been designed so that higher-order thinking not only is engaged but also provides something worthwhile to think about.

GATHERING KNOWLEDGE THROUGH COMPARING

The mental operation of comparing requires that we look for similarities as well as differences. Comparing involves making astute observations of the ways in which items relate to each other and the ways in which they differ. As a consequence of sharpening one's skills in comparing, we learn to make more careful and thoughtful observations and to consider the similarities and differences before drawing conclusions. Making thoughtful comparisons provides us with new insights and awareness, revealing what lies beyond the surface.

1. Compare a Kindle and a book. List as many similarities as you can think of. List as many differences as you can think of.

Courtesy of Selma Wasserman

Courtesy of Selma Wasserman

a. Review your list of similarities and differences. Check to see if you have made any assumptions that go beyond the observable data. Check to see if you have made any value judgments that go beyond the data. Make any revisions you think necessary in your list.

b. Thinking about your comparisons:

- What did you discover when you compared the Kindle and the book that you hadn't known about before? How did making your comparisons lead you to those discoveries?

c. Extending your thinking:

- What are some advantages of using a Kindle? What are your ideas about that?

- Why do you suppose some readers prefer using a Kindle over a book? What are your ideas about it?

- What accounts for some readers choice of using books rather than Kindles? What are your ideas about that?

2. Compare learning a foreign language from a computer program to learning that language in a classroom. List as many similarities and differences as you can.

a. Review your list of similarities and differences. Check to see if you have made any unwarranted assumptions that are not supported by data. Check to see if you have made any value judgments that are not supported by data. Make any revisions you think necessary in your list.

b. Thinking about your comparisons:

- What did you discover about learning from a computer program that you didn't know before you made your comparisons? What did you discover about learning in a classroom that you didn't know before? How did comparing these two forms of learning a new language lead you to make those discoveries?

c. Extending your thinking:

- What do you consider to be some advantages of learning material from a computer program? What assumptions have you made?

- What do you consider some advantages of learning in a classroom? What assumptions have you made?

- If you wanted to study a foreign language, what method would you prefer? How do you explain your choice?

3. Compare the Vietnam War to World War II. List as many similarities and differences as you can think of. Feel free to use a resource if you choose.

   a. Review your list of similarities and differences. Check to see if you have made any assumptions that go beyond the data. Check to see if you have made any value judgments that are not supported by the data. Make any changes you believe necessary in your list.

   b. Thinking about your comparisons:
      • What new insights did you acquire from making those comparisons? How did comparing further support or fail to support your original thinking about these two wars?

   c. Extending your thinking:
      • Based on the data in your comparisons, why do you suppose there were so many people opposed to the Vietnam War?
      • Why do you suppose so many people were in support of World War II?
      • Based on the data in your comparisons, where do you stand with respect to the need for the United States to have engaged in these wars?

For further practice in comparing:
   • COVID-19 and the Spanish flu
   • The French Revolution and the American Revolution
   • Nikola Tesla and Thomas Edison
   • Republicans and Democrats
   • Dollars and euros
   • The British Parliament and the U.S. Congress
   • Van Gogh and Picasso

- Mao Zedong and Stalin
- Jane Austen and Charlotte Bronte
- T. S. Eliot and Robert Frost
- Cricket and baseball

GATHERING KNOWLEDGE THROUGH OBSERVING

Observing involves making a careful examination of what is seen, heard, touched, and perhaps even smelled. Observations permit us to gather data through a variety of senses.

When we observe, we are gathering data with perceptiveness, with acuity, and with accuracy. We then examine our observations so that their accuracy may be assessed. Making observations allows us not only to gather data but also to gain insight into the phenomena being observed. From making those observations, we grow to understand a little more about our worlds.

There are some cautions to be made in the act of observing; we may tend to "read in" to situations what is not actually there—filtering what we see or hear through our own biased perceptual screen. That is, perhaps, why witness statements to a crime have been notoriously unreliable. What's important in observing is to keep close to the data of what is being observed, barring assumptions and value judgments.

This is not as easy as it may sound. But the data suggest that the more one has extended experiences with this process, the more one can be reliably dependent on the accuracy of their observations. Those accurate perceptions are the bases of our knowledge.

1. Make some observations of the prehistoric monument Stonehenge.

   a. Review your list of observations of the monument. See if you have made any assumptions. Check to see if you've made any value judgments. Make any changes necessary in your list of observations.

   b. Thinking about your observations:

Stonehenge. *https://www.gettyimages.com/detail/photo/stonehenge-england -royalty-free-image/569720287?phrase=stonehenge+england&adppopup=true*

- What observations, if any, did you make about the structure? What observations did you make, if any, about the material used in construction? What observations did you make, if any, about the design?

- What observations have you made about the area in which this structure was built?

- How did your observations lead you to a more informed understanding of this monument?

c. Extending your thinking:

- Based on your observations, who might have been responsible for erecting this monument? What hypotheses can you suggest?

- Based on your observations, what you do suppose might be the purpose of this creation? What hypotheses can you suggest?

- Based on your observations, what explains the reasons for erecting the structure in this particular area? What hypotheses can you suggest?

- Based on your observations, what other structures can you think of that are similar to Stonehenge? In what ways are they similar?

2. Make some observations of the photo.

   a. Review your list of observations. Check to see if you have made any assumptions. Check to see if you have made any value judgments. See if there are any changes you need to make in your list of observations.

   b. Thinking about your observations:

      - What observations have you made about the people in the photograph? What observations have you made about what they are doing? What observations have you made about the surrounding area? What other observations have you made?

   c. Extending your thinking:

      - Based on your observations, what hypotheses can you suggest about the story this picture is telling?

      - Based on your observations, what hypotheses can you suggest to describe the facial expression of the mother.

      - Based on your observations, what hypotheses can you suggest about the relationship of the people?

      - Based on your observations, what caption would you give to this picture?

Dorothea Lange: *Migrant Mother*

3. Make some observations about the Picasso painting known as *Guernica*. Write your observations about the painting.

   a. Review your list of observations. What assumptions have you made? What value judgments have you made? Rethink your observations and make any changes you think necessary.

   b. Thinking about your observations:

      • What observations have you made about the figures? What observations have you made about the shapes of the figures? What observations have you made about the feelings evoked by the figures?

Guernica by Picasso

- What observations have you made about the story this work of art tells?

- What observations have you made about what gives this work of art power?

c. Extending your thinking:

- Based on your observations, how do you see this work of art as a masterpiece? What hypotheses can you suggest?

- Based on your observations, what aspects of the image suggest horror? Based on your observations, how did the artist achieve that?

- Based on your observations, how does this work of art compare to others that are considered masterpieces?

- Based on your observations, how did the artist use the artistic form cubism to depict his feelings about the topic portrayed by the painting?

For further practice in observing:

- Make some observations of the film *Casablanca.* How do your observations help you to understand why this has been judged a "classic" film?

- Make some observations of a Hamlet's soliloquy. How do your observations help you to understand how the passage has been crafted? How do your observations help you to understand what gives the passage power?

- Make some observations of a Scrabble board. How do your observations help you to understand how the game is played?

- Make some observations of children playing in a playground. How do your observations help you to understand the nature of the activities? The relationships? The ways in which the children cooperate? The arguments? The skills used in performing the activities?

PROMOTING UNDERSTANDING THROUGH CLASSIFYING

Classifying items allows us to form related groups in which each item in the group has a relationship to the others. When we classify, we organize data in some systematic way, and in doing so, we bring some order to our lives.

Classifying involves two steps: (1) creating the categories and (2) placing the items into the appropriate group. In creating the groups, it is essential that the categories are related to each other. In terms of cognitive difficulty, step 1 is the more difficult, while step 2 requires lower-level skills.

1. Examine the following list of foods. Classify them by putting them into related groups: apple pie, potato salad, salmon, shrimp, roast beef, broccoli, pasta, croissant, bagels, guacamole, risotto, scrambled eggs, ginger ale, orange juice, grapes, lamb chops, hot dogs, gelato, popsicle, corn flakes, potato chips, salsa, tomatoes, arugula, zucchini, turkey leg, hamburgers, fudge, brownies, brie cheese, tuna fish, tomato soup, sausage, bacon, peanut butter, olives.

   a. Review your classification system. How did your groupings help you to understand more about these foods?

b. Thinking about your classifications:

- Which groupings give you added insight into these foods?

- What other groupings might you have made?

- If you were to group the foods according to which need to be stored in a refrigerator and which do not, how would that help you to understand more about the foods?

- If you were to group them according to which need to be prepared and which are eaten without preparation, how would that help you to understand more about the foods?

- If you were to group them according to which are "fattening" and which are not, how would that help you to understand more about the foods?

c. Extending your thinking:

- Why do you suppose we classify foods? In your opinion, what purpose does classifying foods serve?

- How does classifying help us to understand the nature of foods and food products? What are your ideas about that?

- How, in your view, does a supermarket classify foods? What hypotheses can you suggest to explain that classification system?

- In what other ways do classification systems help us to bring order to our lives? What are your ideas about it?

2. Classify the following according to your own criteria: Nova Scotia, Prince Edward Island, Newfoundland, Ontario, Quebec, Manitoba, Alberta, British Columbia, Vancouver Island, Northwest Territories, New Brunswick, Labrador, Yukon, Saskatchewan, Queen Charlotte Islands, Nunavut, Greenland, Iceland.

   a. Review your groupings. Explain how you came to make those groups.

   b. Thinking about your groups:

- How are your groups related to each other?
- What insights did you get about these geographical areas from creating your groups?
- How did making your groups enable you to understand more about these places?

c. Extending your thinking:

- What other groupings might you have made? What purpose would those groupings serve?
- How does the act of classifying enable us to increase our understanding of people, places, and events? What are your ideas about it?
- Suppose you grouped these geographical areas according to their governments? How would that further your understanding of these places? What are your ideas about that?

3. Classify the following: George Washington, John Adams, Thomas Jefferson, James Madison, James Monroe, John Quincy Adams, Andrew Jackson, Martin Van Buren, William Henry Harrison, John Tyler, James Knox Polk, Zachary Taylor, Millard Fillmore, Franklin Pierce, James Buchanan, Abraham Lincoln, Andrew Johnson, Ulysses S. Grant, Rutherford B. Hayes, James Garfield, Chester Arthur, Grover Cleveland, Benjamin Harrison, William McKinley, Theodore Roosevelt, William Howard Taft, Woodrow Wilson, Warren G. Harding, Calvin Coolidge, Herbert Hoover, Franklin Roosevelt, Harry S. Truman, Dwight D. Eisenhower, John F. Kennedy, Lyndon B. Johnson, Richard M. Nixon, Gerald Ford, Jimmy Carter, Ronald Reagan, George H. W. Bush, Bill Clinton, George W. Bush, Barack Obama, Donald Trump, Joe Biden.

a. Review your groupings. Explain how you came to create those groups.

b. Thinking about your groups:

- How are your groups related to each other?
- What insights did you gather about these men from creating those groups?

c. Extending your thinking:
- What other groupings might you have created?
- What purpose would those groupings serve?
- How did classifying help you to understand more about these U.S. presidents?
- Suppose you grouped these men by their contributions to the health and welfare of the country. How would that promote your understanding of their legacy?

For further practice in classifying:
- Classify jobs/work
- Classify musical instruments
- Classify animals
- Classify dogs
- Classify sports
- Classify European countries
- Classify artists
- Classify composers
- Classify tools
- Classify shoes

PROMOTING UNDERSTANDING THROUGH IDENTIFYING ASSUMPTIONS

Assumptions are thoughts, ideas, issues, and statements that we take for granted. Some assumptions that we take for granted turn out to be true. Some turn out to be false. What is important is that we learn to recognize what is assumed—those that we ourselves make and those made by others—since assuming something to be true puts us on shaky ground.

It is when we draw conclusions or take actions based on unwarranted assumptions that we get into trouble. One egregious example of acting on assumptions is the case of the Ponzi scheme—in which investors were promised high returns with little or no risk. Many investors lost fortunes based on faulty assumptions about the legitimacy of the claims before checking to find out their validity.

The roots of prejudice lie in our making assumptions about people based on their skin color, their religious beliefs, their ethnicity, their social class, or their sexual orientation. That is why recognizing and identifying assumptions opens our minds to more thoughtful and more rational behaviors.

1. In 1942, in California, Oregon, Washington, Alaska, and Utah, Japanese Americans, most of whom were U.S. citizens, were rounded up and "evacuated" to internment camps where they would be imprisoned until the end of World War II as a "matter of military necessity." Their personal possessions, homes, cars, property, and businesses were lost or sold at "fire sales" for a fraction of their worth. They were allowed to take with them only what they could carry.

   General DeWitt, who was tasked with enforcing Executive Order 9066, under which the U.S. Army was given blanket power to deal with the "enemy alien problem," stated that the Japanese constituted a "large, unassimilated, tightly knit racial group bound to an enemy nation by strong ties of race, culture, custom and religion."

   a. What assumptions were made by the American government in their incarceration of Japanese American citizens? Identify as many as you can.

   b. Thinking about these assumptions:
      • What assumptions were made about the dangers posed by Japanese Americans living in the coastal areas?

- What assumptions were made about where they lived?
- What assumptions were made about the nature of their ethnicity?
- What assumptions were made about the necessity to intern them?

c. Extending your thinking:

- The fears of Americans led to the internment of Japanese citizens at the beginning of World War II, while German Americans were not subjected to the same treatment. How do you explain this? What assumptions are being made?
- Some Japanese Americans who lived on the East Coast were exempt from incarceration. How do you explain this? What assumptions are being made?
- The rights in the U.S. Constitution that American citizens take for granted did not protect the 110,000 Japanese Americans who were sent to prison camps for four years. How do you explain this? What assumptions are being made?

2. During the COVID-19 crisis, many people chose to disregard medical advice and refused to get vaccinated or wear masks.

a. What assumptions might they have been making? List as many as you believe are at the root of such refusals.

b. Thinking about these assumptions:

- What assumptions were made about the data from which this group of people drew their advice?
- What assumptions were made about the fears they harbored about the vaccines?
- What assumptions were made about the wisdom shown by these people?

- What assumptions were made about the danger these people imposed on others?

c. Extending your thinking:

- What, in your view, explains people's refusals to take protection from infection? What assumptions are being made?

- What, in your view, explains political figures advocating against vaccination? What assumptions are being made?

- What steps should have been taken to ensure that more people got vaccinated? What assumptions are being made?

3. Helen Keller, deaf and blind, given up as "hopeless" when she was a child, was taught to read by her teacher Annie Sullivan. As an adult, Keller became a staunch advocate for the rights of the disabled.

a. What assumptions do we sometimes make about people who have various disabilities? List as many as you have heard about or seen or made yourself.

b. Thinking about assumptions:

- What assumptions are made about the nature of the disability?

- What assumptions are made about the effect of their disability on their lives?

- What assumptions are made about their potential to excel in their chosen activities?

- What assumptions are being made about the way they are treated by others?

- What assumptions are being made about their limitations?

c. Extending your thinking:

- What, in your view, explains an employer's refusal to hire a job applicant because of their disability? What assumptions are being made?

Helen Keller

- What, in your view, explains why children bully other children because of their disabilities? What assumptions are being made?

- What, in your view, explains the need for the passage of the Americans with Disabilities Act (ADA)? What assumptions are being made?

- If two people are applying for the same job, with equal competence, and one is disabled, which should an employer hire? What assumptions are being made?

For further practice in identifying assumptions:

- What assumptions do we make about LGBT people?

- What assumptions do we make when we vote for a particular candidate?
- What assumptions do we make when we purchase a lottery ticket?
- What assumptions do we make when we read a recipe?
- What assumptions were being made when the United States put an embargo on the immigration of Chinese in 1949?
- What assumptions are being made when we purchase a new product online?
- What assumptions are being made when we take something read on the internet as truth?
- What assumptions are being made when an employer hires a new person for a particular job?
- What assumptions were being made by the U.S. government that repeatedly increased the numbers of servicemen sent to Vietnam?
- What assumptions are we making about the increased use of AI?
- Which assumptions are probably true? Which are probably false? How do you know?

PROMOTING UNDERSTANDING THROUGH SUGGESTING HYPOTHESES

The operation of suggesting hypotheses asks us to come up with a variety of possible explanations for a particular question, problem, or dilemma. It involves identifying alternative possibilities as well as determining which explanations have the greatest credibility. In some cases, we may have to test our hypotheses—a step that carries this operation to the next level of difficulty.

When we become more habituated to suggesting hypotheses as a means of trying to figure out an explanation for a problem, it frees us from making dogmatic assertions, from seeing life from only one perspective, and from "black-and-white" judgments. It is a skill that enables us to deal more effectively, with more self-reliance and more independence, in facing the problems we deal with in the normal course of our lives.

1. Make some observations of Da Vinci's famous painting *Mona Lisa*.

   a. Suggest some hypotheses to explain why this painting is considered a masterpiece. What criteria might be used to identify a work of art as a masterpiece? What are your ideas about it?

   b. Thinking about your hypotheses:
      - What hypotheses might be related to the image of the person?
      - What hypotheses might be related to the style of painting?
      - What hypotheses might be related to the feelings evoked by the painting?
      - What other hypotheses can you suggest to explain it?

   c. Extending your thinking:
      - What other paintings do you know about that are considered masterpieces? In what ways do these other paintings compare with *Mona Lisa*?
      - What, in your view, are the criteria used to identify those paintings as masterpieces? What criteria, in your view, should be used?
      - What, in your view, makes this painting worth millions of dollars? What hypotheses can you suggest to explain it?

2. During the serious spread of COVID-19, Fox News host Tucker Carlson used his program to give false information about the vaccines, the need to use masks, and the numbers of people who have died from the infection. In the aftermath, when Carlson was fired from his job at Fox, his colleagues claimed that he knew the information he was spreading was false.

Mona Lisa. *https://www.gettyimages.com/detail/illustration/oil-painting-of-mona-lisa-from-leonardo-da-royalty-free-illustration/1361615560?phrase =mona+lisa+painting&adppopup=true*

a. What do you suppose explains the spread of false information about such an important and life-threatening situation on a news broadcast? What hypotheses can you suggest to explain it?

b. Thinking about your hypotheses:

- Which of your hypotheses seems more likely to be the best explanation? What evidence do you have to support that idea?

- How does hypothesizing help you to understand more about this issue?

- What hypotheses can you suggest to explain how so many listeners were persuaded by false information? How do your hypotheses help you to understand more about this issue?

c. Extending your thinking:

- On TikTok, a news item has been circulating that garnered more than 11 million views. It claimed that the *Titanic* never sank. What hypotheses can you suggest to explain the reason for posting such a "news" item? What hypotheses can you suggest to explain why 11 million viewers tuned into this posting?

- When the Wright brothers built their first airplane and demonstrated the first flying machine, some people were heard to say about flight, "If God wanted men to fly, He would have given us wings." What hypotheses can you suggest to explain such views about new inventions? How does hypothesizing give you greater insight into this issue?

- In Donald Trump's presidential announcement speech (June 16, 2015), he claimed that "Mexicans are, in many cases, criminals, drug dealers, rapists, etc." What hypotheses can you suggest to explain his condemnation of Mexicans? How does hypothesizing give you greater insight into the reasons for his statement?

3. Thomas Edison and Nikola Tesla were contemporaries, inventors, and adversaries who were involved in the "war of the currents"—that is, an argument about whose electrical system would power the world.

   Edison was perhaps better known. He was advocating the use of direct current (DC) for power distribution, for which he held the patents. Tesla, on the other hand, supported alternating current (AC) since he believed it allowed for greater quantities of energy to be transmitted to power large cities. The men, both gifted scientists, were brutal competitors.

   a. What hypotheses can you suggest to explain Edison's resistance to Tesla's position about AC? How do your hypotheses help you to understand more about this issue?

   b. Thinking about your hypotheses:
   - History has shown that it was Tesla "who gave electricity to the world" with AC. He also developed wireless telegraphy, fluorescent lights, remote control, and many more inventions. Yet it is Edison who is better known. How do you explain it? What hypotheses can you suggest?
   - Another brilliant mathematician, Alan Turing, is now acclaimed as the man who built the first computer. His computer was responsible for breaking the Nazis' Enigma code, and he is credited now as one of the men responsible for the defeat of the Nazis during World War II. Yet his name is not generally known. What hypotheses can you suggest to explain it? How do your hypotheses help you to understand more about this issue?

   c. Extending your thinking:
   - Why have cell phones become ubiquitous in our lives? What hypotheses can you suggest to explain it?

- Some people are very concerned about the influence of AI in our lives. Where do you suppose these concerns come from? What hypotheses can you suggest?

- A social media expert suggested that "no child be allowed to be on TikTok under the age of 13." What hypotheses can you suggest that explains this position? How do your hypotheses help you to understand more about this issue?

- Despite an abundance of scientific evidence, there are still some naysayers who do not accept the data about climate change. What hypotheses can you suggest to explain it? How do your hypotheses help you to understand more about this issue?

- The governor of Florida has put a ban books that teach about racial issues in schools. What hypotheses can you suggest to explain his motives? How do your hypotheses help you to understand more about this issue?

For further practice in suggesting hypotheses:

- How do you explain the reason for some children becoming bullies? What hypotheses can you suggest?

- How do you explain what lies behind people's prejudices? What hypotheses can you suggest?

- Josef Stalin was responsible for the millions of deaths and suffering during his long reign as leader of the Soviet Union. Mao Zedong was also responsible for the death of millions of Chinese who died from starvation in the Great Leap Forward. Yet these men were revered at their deaths as heroes. How do you explain this? What hypotheses can you suggest?

- On November 14, 1960, Ruby Bridges, age six, became the first African American child to attend the all-white William Frantz Elementary School. She was escorted to the school by federal marshals. As she walked to the school, she had to pass a mob of hateful protesters who threw rocks and screamed obscenities at her. What hypotheses can you suggest to explain the hostility of the protesters? What hypotheses can you suggest to explain what it takes for a six-year-old to have done this brave act of defiance? How do your hypotheses help you to understand more about these issues?

- Our language usage changes over the years. Generation by generation, pronunciations evolve, new words are borrowed or invented, and the meanings of old words drift. How do you explain it? What hypotheses can you suggest to explain the reasons for such changes in our language usage?

Promoting Understanding through Summarizing

A summary is a brief or condensed statement that delivers the big ideas of an essay, a book, a film, a text, an issue—whatever has been presented. It is a restating of the essence of the matter. It requires conciseness without omitting what is important.

Condensing the significant ideas as to what matters and what is relevant, omitting what is irrelevant, and identifying what is of greater and of lesser significance contributes to the sharpening of one's ability to discriminate.

When we become adept at summarizing, we are more able to discern relevant from irrelevant, significant from insignificant, and consequential from trivial, sharpening our skills and increasing our understanding.

1. Write a caption for this photo.

   a. How, in your opinion, does your caption capture the main idea of the photo? Rethink what you have written and make any changes you think necessary.

   b. Thinking about your summary:
      - How did your summary reflect the animals seen in the photo? What were the compelling features of the animals? How did your summary reflect that?

Newly hatched ducklings. *Courtesy of Selma Wasserman*

- How did your summary reflect the environment of the animals? What was significant about the environment?

- How did your summary include any of the reactions you had to the photo? Why did you think it was necessary to include those reactions in your summary?

c. Extending your thinking:

- How do you suppose those ducklings ended up in a box? What hypotheses can you suggest?

- What kind of story could you write about five ducklings that ended up in a box? Write a short paragraph that would tell that story.

2. The Zimmerman telegram (as seen on page 50), sent in 1917 and intercepted and decoded by the British, revealed a German plan to conduct unrestricted submarine warfare and to form an alliance with Mexico and Japan if the United States declared war on Germany. The message was passed on to the United States. Its publication caused outrage and contributed to the U.S. entry into World War I.

    a. Write a one-sentence summary of the contents of the telegram. Reflect on your summary and consider any changes you think necessary to be sure you have captured the big ideas of the message.

    b. Thinking about your summary:

- How did your summary capture the threat implicit in the message? What key words in the message led you to that understanding?

- What were the key ideas in the message that provoked the United States to war? How did your summary reflect those ideas?

    c. Extending your thinking:

- If you wanted to encode this telegram, how would you go about doing that?

- What might have been some alternatives for the United States other than declaring war? Suggest, in summary form, at least three alternatives to the declaration of war based on the message in the telegram.

- What, in your view, was the true purpose of the Zimmerman telegram? What resources did you use to make that judgment?

3. Write a summary of Darwin's theory of evolution. Summarize his theory in two or three sentences.

Department of State,

Washington, February 26, 1917.

11 am

AMEMBASSY

    MEXICO CITY (MEXICO).

10

    The Department has obtained possession of text of telegram sent by Zimmermann, German Secretary of State, to the German Minister to Mexico, which was sent by way of Washington and, we are informed, was forwarded by Bernstorff on January nineteenth. It states in substance that it is the intention of the German Government to begin unrestricted submarine warfare on February first; that in spite of this plan the German Government will endeavor to keep the United States neutral, but if they do not succeed the German Government make an offer of an alliance with Mexico as follows: To make war together; to make peace together; Germany to give financial aid and to agree that Mexico is to recapture Arizona, Texas, and New Mexico. Settlement of details are left to the German Minister. German Minister is instructed to inform the President of Mexico of this proposal most secretly, as soon as war with United States is certain and to suggest that he should, on his own initiative, approach Japan with some suggestion for an understanding which is not quite clear, and, at the same time, offer to mediate between Japan and Germany. STOP.

    Paragraph. You will at once see General Carranza or, if that cannot be arranged immediately, the Minister of Foreign Affairs. Read

                    to

Zimmerman Telegram

a. Review your summary and check to see if you have included the big ideas of Darwin's theory. Check to see if you have included any irrelevant details. Make any changes you think necessary as you review your summary.

b. Thinking about your summary:

- What do you consider the big ideas of Darwin's theory? Which words in his theory are considered vital elements of the evolutionary cycle?

- What evidence did Darwin use to formulate his theory? How was that evidence obtained? What do you believe to be the validity of that evidence?

c. Extending your thinking:

- Based on your summary, what do you consider to be the implications of the Darwin theory?

- Based on your summary, what do you consider to be any flaws in the theory?

- Based on your summary, why do you suppose there are still people who reject the theory? What hypotheses can you suggest to explain it?

- Based on your summary and your understanding, should Darwin's theory be taught in science classes in school? What evidence supports your ideas?

Promoting Understanding through Interpreting Data

Sherlock Holmes, that fictional master of interpretation, made history by his ability to discern clues that led him to solve the puzzles that others could not unravel. For example, in the *Case of the Curious Incident of the Dog in the Night*, Holmes correctly discerned that the dog did not bark when the horse was stolen. That led Holmes to the interpretation that the culprit was not a stranger but someone the dog recognized.

While perhaps not in the same class as that fictional detective, we interpret data many times a day in the normal course of our lives. We may look at an advertisement for a new washing machine and read the data about it, from which we may draw some conclusions about its durability and worth. We examine an advertisement for a new-generation desktop computer, and we make an interpretation of its quality and its desirability. We listen to an infant's cry, interpret what message the child is sending, and, on the basis of that interpretation, respond in kind.

When we interpret, we look for the meanings in the messages that are being sent, putting meaning into and taking meaning out of a body of data. Sometimes the data are very clear, and making interpretations is relatively easy. Sometimes the data are elusive, and we have to make some inferences that go beyond the data.

We interpret graphs, tables, charts, pictures, cartoons, reports, and jokes. We interpret poetry and prose, nuances of expression, and messages that are sent in any form.

Our ability to interpret with accuracy is dependent on how reliably we "have read" the message. On the other hand, we may misinterpret a message, and this may get us into hot water. For example, we look at a campaign slogan, like MAGA, and we may read into it meanings that are not actually there. When we misinterpret a message, we may be making unwarranted assumptions, going far beyond what the data allow us to conclude.

Sharpening our skills in learning to interpret based on the evidence, reading into a message no more than what the data allow, provides us with more accurate and reliable understandings. When we continually misinterpret, we continue to miss meanings and thus become severely handicapped in our ability to understand.

1. Read the following paragraphs. Then, on the basis of these data alone, write 10 statements that are true based solely on the evidence in the paragraph.

The first railroad, from Liverpool to Manchester, was built in 1830. Before then, most transportation had been via horse-driven coach, which could travel as fast as 10 miles per hour, although only the mail coaches, with their system of horse relays, could maintain that pace. Now with railroads crisscrossing the nation, it was possible to travel at a once-inconceivable 60 miles per hour.

For the system to function, however, arriving and departing trains needed to maintain a strict schedule. The result was a profound change in the way communities thought of time and distance. Prior to the railroad, a village in northwestern England might have had its clocks set at 10 minutes after 7, while a village 100 miles away might have had its clocks set for 20 minutes later. The discrepancy couldn't be noticed when someone traveling via a horse-driven coach required more than 10 hours to go from one village to another.

But now, with trains speeding across that 100 miles in an hour and 40 minutes, the difference between the clocks in those two villages was significant. If similar differences existed in every community, a coordinated departure and arrival schedule would have been impossible. Using the measurement of time as determined by the Royal Greenwich Observatory in London, every railroad clock and soon every other timepiece throughout England was set for the same hour and minute in what became known as Railroad Time (Morrell, 2013).

a. Check your statements against the information in the paragraphs. See if you have made any statements that have gone beyond the data in the paragraphs. Make any changes necessary in your list of statements.

b. Thinking about your interpretations:

- What do your interpretations tell you about how the railroads brought changes to people's lives in England?

- What do you suppose is probably true about the changes brought by the railroads but not borne out by direct evidence? What clues in the paragraphs allow you to make those assumptions?

c. Extending your thinking:

- Based on your reading, what evidence supports the idea that once the first railroad was built, other railroad lines were sure to follow?

- Based on your reading, what evidence supports the idea that horse-drawn coaches used for transportation were soon to be outdated?

- Based on your reading, what evidence supports the idea that the general population was happy with the way communities thought of time and travel?

- Based on your reading, what evidence supports the idea of the necessity of "Railroad Time"?

2. The following is a table that shows the countries of those men and women who won Nobel Prizes in the years 1930–1956.

   a. Write 10 statements that are demonstrably true based on the information in the table on page 55. Reread your statements and compare them to the data in the table to see if they are clearly supported by the information. Make any changes you believe necessary.

   b. Thinking about your interpretations:

      - What were you able to interpret about the country that claimed the most Nobel Prizes during this period of time? What country had the fewest? What can you conclude about these two countries based on the data in the table? What assumptions have you made?

      - Based on the data in the table, is it possible for you to interpret that the reason for the dearth of Nobel Prizes in Russia during these years was because of government control of science innovations?

      - Based on the data in the table, would you be able to interpret that the reason for the large numbers of Nobel Prizes awarded to the U.S. candidates was due to the fact that science is strongly supported by the government?

      - Would you be able to conclude that Nobel Prizes are awarded largely to the most deserving men and

Countries of the Men and Women Who Won Nobel Prizes from 1930 to 1956

	Physics	Chemistry	Medicine	Literature	Peace	Total
1. United States	13	10	20	5	7	55
2. Germany	2	10	5		1	18
3. England	8	3	6	4	4	25
4. France		2		5	2	9
5. Sweden		1	1	2	1	5
6. Switzerland		2	3	1		6
7. Austria	3		1			4
8. Denmark			1	1		2
9. Holland	1			1		2
10. Italy	1			1		2
11. Belgium			1			1
12. Norway						0
13. Spain						0
14. Canada		1				1
15. Russia		1				1
16. Poland						0
17. India	1					1
18. Argentina			1		1	2
19. Finland		1		1		2
20. Chile				2		2
21. Hungary	1		1			2
22. Ireland	1					1
23. Japan	1					1
24. Iceland				1		1
25. Portugal				1		1
26. Puerto Rico				1		1

women? What data in the table allow you to make that interpretation?

- The size of a country and its overall population probably have a great deal to do with the eligible candidates for

Nobel Prizes. Based on the data in the table, would you say this was true, probably true, or false?

c. Extending your thinking:

- What interpretations can you draw from the data in the table? What other kinds of information do you need to support your statements?

- Based on the information in the table, what interpretations can you make about how the Nobel Prize committee makes its determinations?

- Based on the information in the table, what interpretations can you make about why some countries produce more Nobel Prizes and others produce few or none?

3. Morality police are a special group that enforces Islamic moral codes. Iran's morality police aren't the world's only Islamic religious police. A few countries in the Middle East and Southeast Asia have police devoted to tracking down and punishing "un-Islamic" activities.

Such countries have criminalized behaviors, including drinking alcohol, social mixing of unrelated men and women, sex outside of marriage, sex between people of the same gender, skipping prayers, and wearing types of clothing considered immodest. Women are more often charged with offenses about their dress and face fines and imprisonment as well as traditional Sharia-based sentences, such as caning, beatings, amputations, death by stoning, and public execution.

1. Based on your reading of the paragraphs about the morality police, what can you say, with certainty, about their role in certain Islamic societies?

a. Review your statements. See if you have made any that have gone beyond the data in the paragraphs. Make any corrections you believe necessary.

b. Thinking about your interpretations:

- What can you deduce, with a measure of certainty, about the role of the morality police?

- What can you deduce, with a measure of certainty, about the need for morality police in the Islamic culture?

- What can you deduce, with a measure of certainty, about the behaviors that are considered criminal in the Islamic culture?

- What can you deduce as "probably true" that women are more subject to these punishments than men?

c. Extending your thinking:

- Based on your interpretations, what do you see as the reasons for such a special police force in the Islamic culture?

- Based on your interpretations, what do you see as some important consequences of such morality laws?

- Based on your interpretations, who decides what are considered "un-Islamic" activities? How, in your view, did such rules and regulations arise? Why, in your view, is this a reflection of Islamic culture and not, for example, of other religions?

CHAPTER 6

Sharpening Your Thinking Skills

Applying What Is Known to Practice

THIS SECTION ON THOSE HIGHER-ORDER THINKING SKILLS THAT involve applications to practice includes four categories of activities: applying knowledge to designing projects and investigations, problem solving, applying what is known to making decisions, and creating and inventing. In each section, three increasingly difficult activities are included. The objective in these activities is to reflect on appropriate courses of action, appropriate responses, and appropriate strategies in bringing your responses to a considered conclusion.

In each situation, you are asked to reconsider your responses through your own critical eye and make whatever adjustments you believe necessary. As in the group of activities in chapter 5, there are no right answers, no right methods. It is the quality of your thinking that is the objective of this work.

APPLYING KNOWLEDGE TO DESIGNING PROJECTS AND INVESTIGATIONS

While designing investigations is generally attributed to what scientists do in laboratories, in fact, we, as a general rule, do much of this in our homes and workplaces, although we might call those actions by a different name.

To take a mundane example, planning a dinner party involves a considerable amount of organizing and then creating and carrying out strategies that ensure its success. Planning a holiday trip with family is another example. A group of teenagers took it on themselves to mount a campaign to help their dying small town transform itself into a viable economic success. Planning a large wedding also involves considerable thoughtfulness, useful strategies, and not a small amount of creative thinking.

Initiating a campaign to promote recycling in one's neighborhood, developing a fund-raising plan to help the local library, developing a successful training program to teach your dog obedience, or creating a plan to help a new immigrant family to feel more welcome in their new town are some other examples of how, in the daily course of our lives, we take on projects and investigations that are intended to solve problems we face as friends, neighbors, and citizens.

To make these tasks clearer, it will be easily seen that designing projects and investigations incorporates several of the previously mentioned mental operations: observing, comparing, gathering and organizing information, classifying, and interpreting data, to name a few. It would be fair to say that the more successful one is in carrying out these subset mental operations, the more effective will be the results in these more complex situations.

How does this kind of work enable us to become more intelligent consumers of information? While the means and ends are not obvious, it is the case that when we do engage in them, the clear result is a sharpening of the intellect, a habituation to the process of data gathering, selecting what is relevant, substantive, and true and selecting out what is irrelevant, unsubstantial, and false.

When we undertake to design a project or carry out an investigation, we first need to be clear about what we wish to do; that is, the clearer the objective, the more what follows will make sense and provide the "road map" for the development of the plan. Needless to say, work in this area requires a higher level of cognitive sophistication because there is no one way to solve a problem, design a project, or carry out an investigation. But experience has shown that the ability to succeed is within our grasp.

It is not a given, but an added thought is this: experience with designing projects and carrying out investigations is much enriched when two people, of like mind, can work together. There is much to be gained from the exchange of ideas and strategies and much to be learned from each other's insights. Besides, it is often more enjoyable to work with a like-minded chum than it is alone.

As you begin work in this area, you may wish to start with a tentative plan, similar to a road map or a storyboard, before moving ahead to action. It is not a requirement; some prefer to just jump in. No single way is recommended, as people with varying skills and aptitudes will find their best ways.

1. In the years 1838–1841, Ludwig Semmelweis discovered that the reason so many mothers died from "childbed fever" after childbirth was due to the infections spread by doctors whose unwashed hands carried infectious diseases. There was considerable resistance to Semmelweis's discovery; doctors mocked his ideas, believing that the dried blood on their hands was a mark of their expertise as surgeons.

   a. Design an investigation that would explain how Semmelweis made his discovery and the resulting opposition to his findings. Feel free to use any resources that would inform your work. Then recheck carefully to make sure that your data are accurate and that you have not made any value judgments.

   b. Thinking about your investigation:
   - Create a storyboard to show how the medical profession advanced in their thinking about infection since Semmelweis's time. What data have you gathered to show who were the significant people responsible for those advances?
   - Based on the data you have gathered, what, in your view, do you consider the main contributions to those advances? Based on the data you have gathered, what, in your view, do you consider the main objections to these advances? Create an outline that highlights the relevant information.

- Based on the data you have gathered, what do you consider the significant factors that impede advances in science? Check your work and make sure you have identified those value judgments you've made.

c. Extending your thinking:

- Gather some data and design an investigation to demonstrate how Darwin faced similar protests about his work as did Semmelweis. What were some similarities in those objections? What were some differences?

- Gather some data and design an investigation to demonstrate how Freud faced similar protests about his work as did Semmelweis. What were some similarities in those objections? What were some differences?

- Gather some data and design an investigation to demonstrate how Galileo faced similar protests about his work? What were some similarities in those objections? What were some differences?

- Gather some data and design an investigation to document the rationale behind the protests and objections to face masks and vaccinations in the face of the COVID-19 pandemic. What do the data say about some of the reasons for those objections? How are they similar to/different from those faced by Galileo, Freud, Darwin, and Semmelweis?

2. In the late 19th and early 20th centuries, the United States and Canada established what were called "residential schools" for the housing and the education of indigenous children. The implicit goal of the schools was essentially the "cultural extermination of indigenous people."

The reality of the situation was that children were forcibly removed from their homes—and placed in centers that were more like asylums, many of them run by the Catholic Church. The conditions that were created were responsible for the deaths of indigenous children, many thousands of whom were murdered by harsh treatment, excessive punishment, and lack of medical care. Hundreds of unmarked graves were found, many years later, on school grounds.

More than 150,000 children were taken from their homes and placed in distant boarding schools where the focus was on manual labor, religious instruction, and cultural assimilation. In retrospect, this has been called "cultural genocide."

a. Do some investigations about the residential schools in the United States and Canada. Use whatever resources you can find to give you the background information you need. Use the information you gathered to design an investigation to show the tribes from which children were taken and the methods of education provided to assimilate them into the mainstream culture. Check your work for value judgments and assumptions. Make any changes you believe necessary in order to ensure that what you have written is factually correct.

b. Thinking about your investigation:

- Based on your research, what do you consider the important reasons for the creation of residential schools for indigenous children?

- What do you see as the justifications that permitted these children to be removed from their homes? What laws sanctioned this?

- What do you consider to be the rationale behind the punishing treatment of the children in the schools? What hypotheses can you suggest to explain it?

- How, in your view, should these survivors be compensated for what was done to them by U.S. and Canadian authorities?

c. Extending your thinking:

- Given the data you have gathered, what do you consider to be some of the "emotional scars" that these adults carry as a result of their treatment at the residential schools?

- How should the federal authorities of both the United States and Canada be held to account for the treatment of these children? What are your ideas about that?

- Do some more research to find out about any other groups of children that were removed from their homes to undergo enforced education. What do you conclude was the rationale behind such initiatives?

3. Do an investigation in which you interview at least 12 children under the age of 10 to ask them about their use of tablets. Before you begin your interviews, arm yourself with a list of questions that you want to raise with them. And be sure to have a means of recording their responses.

a. Review the responses made by the children. Make a note of which questions provided the best information and which questions provided less helpful responses. Review your list of questions and make any changes you think would benefit the data acquisition.

b. Thinking about your investigation:
    - What did the data you gathered reveal about the children's use of tablets? What did the data reveal about how much time children spend on their tablets? What did the data reveal about what the children believed they were learning from their tablet work?

    - What did the data reveal about any restrictions that parents placed on children's use of the tablets?

    - What did the data reveal about the use of tablets in school situations?

c. Extending your thinking:

- Based on your investigations, what conclusions were you able to draw about children's use of tablets?

- Based on your investigations, what conclusions were you able to draw about whether tablets are an effective learning tool?

- Based on your investigations, what conclusions were you able to draw about any damaging effects of tablet use on children under 10 years of age?

- On reflection, what would you change if you were going to do this task again?

- Based on your investigations, how would you summarize your findings in a short paragraph?

APPLYING WHAT IS KNOWN TO PROBLEM SOLVING

The process of problem solving incorporates several other operations, including hypothesizing; collecting, organizing, and interpreting data; and evaluating results. Not all of these sub-steps are involved in the solution of every problem. It is also important to note that there is no single problem-solving method that can be applied to every problem.

Problems come in all sizes and shapes; some are of epic proportions, and some can be dealt with by using limited resources and limited energy. Epic problems are like octopuses, with many tentacles, requiring different sets of strategies. These mega problems require identifying the different parts that lead, eventually, to the action dictated by the plan.

For example, if you were going to problem solve how to create the best pizza with the limited resources in your home kitchen, that would be an activity that would be considerably less challenging than planning the D-Day attack on the European continent during World War II. The former would involve fewer steps with considerably less at stake if the attempt failed. In either case, there would be levels of stress connected with taking on the problem—and stress levels would vary based not only on the nature of the problem but also on one's sense of their own expertise in that problem area.

At the outset, it would be helpful that the problem and/or the parts be clearly defined and understood. When the problem is not clear at the outset, solutions may be inappropriate, inadequate, or simply wrong. You will also need to figure out what information you need as you begin to work out a plan of action. In addition, you will need to determine the accuracy and reliability of the information.

In the normal course of a day's activities, we face many problems that require higher-order thinking that leads to a course of action. Some of these are easily addressed; others are more complex and defy simple solutions. Sharpening our skills as problem solvers gives us an important edge: we can face the unknown with some small degree of confidence in our own ability to figure things out for ourselves. We are less likely to fall into the trap of "means–ends" confusion—where actions are incompatible with our goals, resulting in not only time wasted but also unsatisfying consequences for our hard work.

Skillful problem solvers are the antithesis of those adults who are dependent on others for advice or for help with what needs to be done; they are the antithesis of those who cannot figure out a way to reach a desired goal. They are the antithesis of those who are "stuck"—who need help with even the smallest and most mundane decision before acting.

The three activities that follow are not arranged according to levels of difficulty; each presents its own challenges—easier for some, more difficult for others. Each is representative of a real problem.

1. The problem of the dying goslings.

   Claudia lived on the top floor of an eight-story building, adjacent to a large city park. As the weather turned to spring, she went out to the roof deck to check on the plants and discovered that a Canada goose had nestled among the bushes, sitting on eggs. A few weeks later, the eggs had hatched, and five tiny goslings, looking like balls of yellow fluff, were waddling around the roof deck in a fruitless search for food and water. Apparently, the mother goose had abandoned them as soon as the eggs hatched.

   Claudia knew that the goslings had no chance to survive on their own; if they were not fed and watered, they would likely die.

What plan of action might she take if the goslings were to be saved? Or should she let them die a natural death? Or?

a. How would you describe the problem that Claudia was facing? What values underlie the statement of the problem? If you were in Claudia's position, what statement would you make to describe the problem as you saw it?

b. Thinking about your problem statement:

- What assumptions have you made about the possibility of the return of the mother goose?

- What assumptions have you made about the need to help the goslings survive?

- What hypotheses can you suggest that might explain the behavior of the mother goose?

- Should humans intervene to save an animal or animals in peril? What values do you have that underlie that position?

c. Extending your thinking:

- If your plan is to help save the goslings, what steps would you take to do that?

- What assumptions have you made about any of those steps involved in the rescue?

- If you managed to capture the goslings and remove them, what would be your next steps? What assumptions are you making about the viability of that plan?

- What, if anything, have you found out about how parent geese protect their young? How do the data inform your plan?

2. The problem of the Thanksgiving dinner party.

It was Maddy's turn this year to have her and her husband's family over for Thanksgiving dinner. It was not a holiday she was looking forward to. In the first place, she was not a great cook, and shopping and preparing a large dinner for 12 was daunting. But her husband offered to help—if she would give him specific jobs that he could do on his own.

Second, Maddy knew that there was tension in the two sides of the family. Rob's parents were on the far right of the political spectrum and could be extreme in expressing their views. Maddy's parents were to the left of liberal, and they too could be insistent and stentorian in their pronouncements. Maddy remembered that previous Thanksgiving dinners had ended up in angrily departing guests. How could that be avoided this year?

a. Based on the brief story above, what do you see as the major problems facing Maddy this year? Be specific in identifying those problems. Be cautious about any assumptions being made.

b. Thinking about your problem statements:

- What assumptions have you made about the menu for the dinner?

- What assumptions have you made about the help being offered by Rob?

- What assumptions have you made about Maddy's expertise as a chef?

- What assumptions have you made about the guests?

- What assumptions have you made about how to bring harmony among groups of people with diverse points of view?

c. Extending your thinking:

- What would be a viable plan for the preparation of the dinner? What assumptions are you making about that?

- What would be a viable plan for getting some help in the preparation of the dinner? What assumptions are you making about that?

- What would be a viable plan for a more harmonious gathering of folks of strongly differing opinions? What assumptions are you making about that?

- What would you consider to be some evidence of the effectiveness of your plan? What might stand in the way of the effectiveness of your plan? How, in advance, might you guard against any impediments?

3. Alan's father, having recently lost his wife of 60 years, decided that life on his own was too much for him to handle. With the aid and support of his children, he repaired to a retirement home where he would be among age-alike men and women, have access to some moderate and physically undemanding sports, have his meals prepared, and have a respite for his loneliness. But his positive views were supplanted by disillusionment; life in that retirement home was not happily ever after.

   To help his father deal with his new situation and to give him some new purpose in his life, Alan bought him a laptop computer. Alan thought that learning to use a computer and hooking up to the internet might give his dad some purposeful activities and open new vistas for him.

   Alan was not prepared for his father's response: "Are you kidding me? I'm too old for that stuff."

   a. What is your perception of the problems that Alan faced with respect to his father? Identify them. And as you reflect on your statements, check to see if you have made any assumptions. Make any changes you believe necessary in your problem statements.

   b. Thinking about your problem statements:

   - What observations have you made about Alan's father? How did those observations lead to your problem statement?

   - What observations have you made about Alan? How did those observations lead to your problem statement?

69

- What observations have you made about the retirement home? How did those observations lead to your problem statement?

- What assumptions have you made about Alan? His father? The gift of a computer?

c. Extending your thinking:

- Based on your reading and your problem statements, what would you advise Alan to do with respect to his father's response?

- Based on your reading and your problem statements, what would you advise Alan to do with respect to helping his father get over his rejection of learning to use a computer?

- Based on your reading and your problem statements, how would you go about helping a reluctant learner face the challenges of a new device like a computer?

- Based on your reading and your problem statements, what would you use as evidence that your strategies were effective?

APPLYING WHAT IS KNOWN TO MAKING DECISIONS

When humans were just climbing down from the trees, the lives they led required few decisions—most of which were rooted in the need to find food, to find shelter, and to find a way to protect themselves from not only the elements but also from warring tribes. As civilization progressed, as humans moved forward from the invention of the wheel, to the Industrial Age, and to artificial intelligence, the decisions we face are more complex, more harrowing, and perhaps more significant.

One of the reasons for that is that our lives have become increasingly complicated. A more elusive reason is that we have so many more options from which to choose that the process of choosing becomes more daunting. In a society like ours, where freedom of choice is one of the basic tenets of our lives, sometimes that wide array of choices leaves us perplexed, confused, and overwhelmed. Perhaps that is one reason for those letters to "Agony Aunts"—newspaper editors who receive and respond daily to writers' dilemmas about "what should I do?"

The easy answer is that data inform our choices, as do our values. If we have good data, we have the grounds for making better choices. If we know what values we hold dear and what's important to us, those values inform our choices. But who among us will be the first to claim that they have good information? Or that disinformation or "alternative facts" support a choice? Who among us will be the first to claim that they are clear about what values they hold dear and what's more important to them in their lives?

In most instances, decision making is a very personal act. In some cases, it's an act that can have great relevance to our lives, with consequences that shape our future. In such cases, decisions should be weighed and reflected on, consequences considered, and values that support our choices made clear. When these processes are "in play," the chances are good that the decisions we make are not only wise and informed but also of considerable benefit to ourselves. When we decide impulsively without considering the data or when high emotions rule our choices, the decisions we make could have undesirable, unwarranted, and even dangerous consequences.

One of the dangers in decision making is the way the "institutional press" of a particular group takes over reason and exerts its own agenda to act. Each individual is overpowered by the energy of the crowd; individual decisions are crushed by the powerful pull of the masses. When one joins a crowd, they, in fact, give up all of their individual agency and their rationality. According to Davies (2019), crowds are motivated by feelings that are substituted for reason.

The benefits of making sound and wise decisions on our own hardly needs mention; if we give over our own decision-making prerogatives to others to tell us "what to do," we lose our independence and our freedom to act as individuals. If we lose our capacity to make informed decisions, we are in danger of facing consequences that may be fruitless or, at worst, harmful.

Because decisions of consequence are personal to us, the following three activities cannot possibly address those personal factors for each reader. Instead, they are offered for generic practice where choices are made; the exercise is to use them as "practice tasks" of how good information and personal values may inform personal choice.

1. During the two years in which the threat of COVID-19 imposed a quarantine on many of our out-of-house activities, many people felt adrift—cut off from school, work, recreation, and contact with friends and family. As a consequence, some suffered from acute feelings of depression and other symptoms of distress.

   a. What decisions might a person make in order to avert some of the feelings of isolation during the two years of self-imposed quarantine? Make some statements that would describe those decisions.

   b. Thinking about your decisions:
      - Reexamine each of your decision statements. What data support each of them?
      - What important values of yours lie behind those decisions? Make a list of what you consider to be of importance in each of those decisions.

   c. Extending your thinking:
      - Reexamine each of your decision statements. For each, ask yourself:
        - Is this good?
        - Would I be glad to do it?
        - How will I feel after I have done it?
        - What might be some consequences of this action?
      - After asking yourself these questions, are there any decisions you might want to change?
      - If a friend or relative asked you for advice about what they should do in a similar situation, how would you advise them?

2. In a social gathering, a man you know was bragging to you about something he did that you found abhorrent. In his telling of his story, he seemed to feel no sense of guilt or shame; in fact, he seemed to be happy that he was able to do this and get away with it.

   a. What would you say to this man in response? What data would inform your response? What values do you hold dear that would underlie your response?

   b. Thinking about your decision:
      • Would the nature of his act have an impact on your decision? That is, would certain acts of his be found more tolerable and others more repugnant? Which acts would you find more tolerable? Which more repugnant?
      • Would a nonresponse be acceptable to you? What values that you hold dear would underlie a nonresponse?
      • What do you see as some consequences of the decisions you might choose to make?
      • What do you imagine the man's response might be to one or more of your decisions to act? What data inform your ideas?

   c. Extending your thinking:
      • For each suggested decision, ask yourself:
         • How did I feel about that choice?
         • Was I glad to have done that?
         • How would I feel in retrospect?
         • What might be some consequences of what I did?
      • If a friend asked you for advice about what they should do in a similar situation, how would you advise them?

3. A small group of parents at Sunnyside Elementary School have initiated a proposal to remove certain books from the school library. The books named by them are popular with the children, but the

parents have insisted that they corrupt children's values and teach them things they should not know. The books the parents want banned deal primarily with racism, gender, and sexuality.

a. As a parent, you are opposed to such book banning in the school library. What might you do to oppose the banning of these books? What data might inform your decision? What values do you hold dear that would underlie your decision?

b. Thinking about your decision:

- How can you decide if this is an important issue for you? How does the matter of importance contribute to any action you might take?

- Would the kinds of books to be banned make a difference to you? In your view, should any books be banned from school libraries? If so, which kinds of books would you put on that list?

- What hypotheses can you suggest that would help you to understand why some parents are so eager to see certain books off the school library shelves? As you see it, what values underlie their decisions?

- If some parents opposed to book banning wanted to band together to make a protest to the school board, would you join that group? What kinds of protests would you be in favor of? What kinds of protests would you be opposed to?

c. Extending your thinking:

- Should parents play an active role in making determinations about what books should be allowed in a school library? Where do you stand on this issue? What values underlie your decision?

- What guidelines for parents would you suggest about how their choices should inform the kinds of materials allowed in schools?

- According to your own values, what topics, if any, should be omitted from school curricula? What data inform your choices? What do you see as some consequences of the omission of those topics?

CREATING AND INVENTING

There is a temptation to think of creating and inventing—"playing around"—as frivolous activities—things to do when all our important work is finished. Such beliefs about work and play permeate our adult lives. The achievement-oriented workaholic is a role model; the dreamer is patronizingly tolerated. When we do play, we seem to have to give ourselves permission to do so. And sometimes we feel that we have "earned the right" to play only when the day's work is done. These value systems about work and play are as deeply entrenched as almost any other values we hold.

Yet, in spite of that, we do know that from creating and inventing, both considered part and parcel of "playing" or, more crudely, "messing around," come landmark new creations, innovations, and earth-shattering changes in our lives, in how we think, and in how we behave. From such "messing around" comes the generation of new ideas, new systems, and new technologies. Without creating and inventing, we would never have the electric light, the first computer, or the internet. In fact, it would not be an exaggeration to claim that most of what is new comes from the inventions of generative and creative minds.

It was the physicist Richard Feynman who gave perhaps the most telling description of the importance of "playing around" that led to his Nobel Prize. In his classic book *Surely, You're Joking, Mr. Feynman* (1985), he wrote about how that came to be:

> When my work in physics began to bore me, giving me no pleasure, I taught myself to play with physics, doing whatever I felt like doing not because it was important but because it was interesting and fun for me to play with. So in the Cornell cafeteria I began to play with the dinner plates, tossing them up in the air and observing the "wobble rate."

It was effortless. It was easy to play with those things. It was like uncorking a bottle. Everything flowed out effortlessly. I almost tried to resist it! There was no importance to what I was doing, but ultimately there was. The diagrams and the whole business that I got the Nobel Prize for came from that piddling around with the wobbling plates.

This is not to suggest that any act of creating and inventing will ensure a Nobel Prize in your future. But if we allow ourselves to cultivate the art of play in our lives, to allow us to create and invent not because it's important but because it's fun and interesting, then we have a greater chance to hold on to our self-initiating behaviors, our capacity for risk-taking, and our inventiveness. We are less likely to spend our considerably increased leisure time watching game shows on TV because we have not adequately developed those self-initiating resources.

A recent issue of the "Sunday Opinion" section of the *New York Times* (July 16, 2023) featured an article about the "epidemic of loneliness in the United States," which so far has defied the efforts of scientists and clinicians to find a solution. The article reported that more than one-fifth of Americans over 18 say they often or always feel lonely or socially isolated.

Although in and of itself this would be a sad commentary on their lives, the worst news is that such feelings of social isolation have been linked to various adverse physical and psychological effects, including "increased risk of dementia and heart disease, depression, grief, anxiety." Medical practitioners are of a mixed mind about treatment; drugs, at first, seemed to be the treatment of choice. But in later investigations, "it was found that social connections could be boosted more naturally, with activities like walking, meditation, time spent in nature—small changes that can have a profound influence on the quality of our lives."

It may be a reach to suggest that time spent in playful and creative activities might also contribute substantially to not only improved quality of lives, but also in ways that challenge our intelligent habits of mind. Consider what it must have been like for the first people on Earth to have invented the wheel and seen how much it improved carrying large loads or when William Shakespeare dipped his quill into a pot of ink and created *Hamlet*.

What must have it been like to have seen that the first computer designed by Alan Turing was able to decipher the Enigma code of the Nazis, contributing substantially to the shortening of World War II? What was it like when Alexander Graham Bell heard the first voice over the new machine he invented that he called the telephone or when Wilbur and Orville Wright saw their first plane take off into the sky? All that tinkering around in garages and homemade laboratories paid off in spades, and lives were irrevocably changed.

How much "messing around" did these people have to do? And how long was it before they were able to see the success of their efforts? When one is hard at work at creating and inventing, there is little time to feel lonely or socially isolated. One becomes so immersed and so satisfied with the act of creating that that is all that matters. In fact, life becomes purposeful—and that perhaps is the key word.

Ask a writer, a painter, a sculptor, a poet, a chef, an engineer, or an architect if they feel lonely during the act of creating and inventing something new. Of course, there is frustration when what a creator or inventor is working on fails to deliver on its promise. But the joy of the creative process, with the mind constantly engaged, doesn't diminish. It is almost as if the success of one's efforts barely matches the pleasure that comes from the engagement in the process.

Creating and inventing may be one of the most joyful and pleasurable of the many higher-order thinking skills that can inform and enrich our lives.

The following three "creating and inventing" activities provide an opportunity for you to experience what it feels like to be inside the creative act and to feel the generative spirit that is part of what comes from your mind. There's no guarantee that you will find it enjoyable at the outset; often it takes courage, a lot of perseverance, and dedication to create something new. But when you can experience that joy in the process and what results when you can step back and see what you have done, you will have felt what other creators have felt. Or as Stephen Sondheim wrote, putting words into the mouth of George Seurat, "I made a hat where there never was a hat" (*Sunday in the Park with George*).

1. Creating and inventing a story.

   A recent news article told of a sea otter, recently released into the Pacific Ocean from the Monterey Bay Aquarium, that began to make mischief by attacking people on surfboards, flipping their boards, and taking them over to ride the waves itself. The newspapers referred to the otter's escapades as "boardjacking." While the surfers were not exactly pleased to have their boards taken, leaving them to swim to shore, many crowds gathered to enjoy watching the otter, a natural surfer, cavort on the high seas.

   From this news story, create a children's book for ages six to eight.

   a. Review your story. Make any editorial changes you believe are needed to meet the criterion of what children of that age might be able to read and enjoy.

   b. Thinking about your story:
      - What features of the story made it humorous? Sad? Interesting for children?
      - How did you portray the otter to "bring it to life"?
      - On reflection, what might you change to give it more appeal?

   c. Extending your thinking:
      - What did you find difficult about creating a story for children?
      - How did you overcome those difficulties?
      - What makes writing a story hard for you?

2. Creating and inventing what men will be wearing in the year 2523.

   It is no secret that styles of clothing change with the times. Two hundred years ago, men wore tight-fitting pantaloons and knee breeches, buckled shoes, short-fronted tailcoats and fitted waistcoats, linen shirts with frills, and linen underdrawers. These styles evolved over the years to what is now considered the height of fashion for men.

What will men's clothing styles look like 500 years from now? How might environmental issues impact those clothes? What might be "fashionable" for men in 2523?

Make some illustrations of men's clothing styles as you think they might appear in the future.

a. Review the images of your clothing designs. What assumptions have you made about the quality of life in 2523? How did those assumptions influence your design?

b. Thinking about clothing designs:

- What, in your view, explains the changes in clothing designs for men and women over the centuries?

- Who, in your view, has the greatest influence on the design of clothing?

- How, in your view, do these designs become so popular?

c. Extending your thinking:

- How do you explain the fact that once a design becomes "in vogue," it is considered gauche to wear anything different?

- How do you explain the fact that clothing designed by a famous fashion designer costs considerably more money than a copy of the same design?

- What, in your opinion, is the life of a fashion designer like? Imagine a scenario in the day of the life of a high-fashion designer. Write a poem about it.

3. Some of your favorite literary characters are invited to a dinner party at your home. You want to make a special dinner for them—all created in your own kitchen. Who are those characters (dead or

alive)? How would you go about finding out what foods they might enjoy? Create a menu that would highlight not only their preferred culinary tastes but also what you believe you might undertake using your own skills.

a. Review your list of favorite characters. What about them makes them favorites of yours? Add or delete any names to make any changes you wish.

b. Thinking about your choices:

- What, if anything, did you discover about any food preferences among your characters?

- What, if anything, did you discover about any food allergies?

- What, if anything, did you discover about any food restrictions (e.g., Vegan? Low calorie? Kosher? Halal?). What changes in your menu need to be made to accommodate those restrictions?

c. Extending your thinking:

- If your characters come from the mid-18th century, how might that alter your menu choices?

- If your menu contains hard-to-get ingredients, how might that alter your choices?

- If your menu contains recipes and/or foods that are complex to make, how do you plan to organize the cooking of the meal so that everything is ready on time and served at the appropriate temperature?

CHAPTER 7

Reflecting on Action

Evaluation without Tears

ALTHOUGH IT MAY SEEM AN EXAGGERATION, IT IS MORE TRUE THAN WE, perhaps, would like to admit. But the simple act of judging—evaluating—is so common that most of us, adults as well as children, make judgments without a second thought.

Is it good? Is it fresh? Is it safer to go by bus or by train? Did you enjoy the movie? I prefer reading history more than biography. That hairstyle looks good on her. My favorite film star is Meryl Streep. I don't know why, but I hate coconut. Carbonated drinks are bad for your health. I can't say enough good things about my dog. He's a great teacher; take a course with him if you can. Kids should have their time on their devices restricted lest they become hopeless tablet junkies. School libraries should not have books about the evils of slavery in the American South.

Now, with a simple click of the mouse, any person with a Facebook page can make a judgment without having considered the implications, the criteria for assessment, or the consequences. We are invited to "like" freely—no matter the weight of that judgment. That very act of "clicking" reduces the important act of judgment to a simplistic, thoughtless gesture.

Ask anyone who has spent any time in school if they can recall the harsh judgments made on their papers, on their behavior, or on their performance in class. Ask anyone who has grown up in a home with well-meaning parents if they have heard or felt acclaim or criticism as a frequent element in their growth and development. Judgments are a constant in one's life, whether we are students, teachers, artists, or just ordinary people walking the paths of life. If we are unlucky, we bear the brunt of those judgments all of our lives.

In the best of circumstances, making judgments is a process that should provide feedback to us—children or adults—that enables our subsequent growth and development. When it is enabling, it is affirming rather than punishing, respectful of ourselves and protective of our dignity, consonant with the criteria for making that judgment, and clear about how we have met or failed to meet those standards. When judgments are helpful, they enable us to take the next steps in what we are learning or doing. When they are hurtful, delivered sometimes with well-meaning intentions, they can linger, like a bad smell that permeates lives for a lifetime (Wassermann 2020).

The truth about making judgments is that they are not truths. They come from the personal perspectives of the evaluators. They are opinions that lie in the eyes of the beholders. What they rest on are not only personal values and personal ideas of what is good but also the evaluator's sense of what meets current and ethical standards. Perhaps that explains the fact that, for example, J. K. Rowling got 17 rejections for her submission of her first Harry Potter manuscript before it was accepted for publication. And the result of that supreme error of judgment is now history.

Accepting the fact that judgments depend on "where one sits on the medicine wheel," that they are variable and change with the times, that they are inconsistent and sometimes arbitrary, that they can be hurtful and punishing, and that they have nothing to do with truth—what is the place of evaluation in a book about developing intelligent habits of mind?

On an old country road, a sign to pedestrians at a street-level railroad crossing says, "Stop! Look! And Listen!" Let those cautionary words be a paradigm for anyone who is venturing forth to make a judgment. Think about the framing of the words and about the "weight" they are going to carry to the person on the receiving end. Think too about the potential consequences of what is being said in judgment on the receiver. Think again about where your judgment is coming from: Your values? Your vested interests? Your ego needs to acclaim yourself superior? Your moral right to make that judgment? Think about how your judgment may help the person take the next steps in their actions or in the framing of their ideas. Think about taming your impulse to punish in making your judgment.

At the very least, take the time to think about the judgment you are making not only with regard to the above criteria but also in terms of the way you utter your judgment. Tone of voice? Facial gestures? Hand gestures? Any other signs of displeasure that underlie the words? Consider too how to deliver any criticism with kindness so that it comes across as helpful rather than hurtful.

Given this long preamble to the activities, the important question is, Why should you take the time to practice becoming more expert in framing your judgmental responses? What's the payoff for you?

In the first instance, there is payoff for the increased development of your intellectual habits of mind when it comes to framing judgments. When you have to think, carefully and respectfully, about what is being said, there is considerable "brain activity" to be exercised. In the second instance, there is substantial benefit to being a person who can relate, thoughtfully and with care, to others in offering an opinion, a point of view, or a position about an issue. Better human relationships are built on the additive responses of people toward each other. Is this sufficient to warrant your practice in these higher-order intellectual skills?

The following activities have been included because they are deliberately provocative—presenting issues that are current, at the time of this writing, and that ask for personal judgments to be made, giving each reader an opportunity not only to reflect on how a judgment is made but also to search for those personal values and the data that underlie those judgments. Being aware of one's values and the data that support those opinions should be enlightening as well as informative.

1. There has been recent news about some of the members on the U.S. Supreme Court accepting "favors" from supporters to their roles on the bench. For example, Justice Clarence Thomas accepted luxury trips and vacations from a billionaire Republican donor. These favors and gifts have come under public scrutiny, given that

such gifts may influence a judge's opinions on certain cases that defer to the positions of their donors.

a. Should Congress play an active role in regulating the ethics of the members of the Supreme Court? Justice Alito claims that Congress has no right to do this.

- What judgments would you make about whether Supreme Court justices may accept "favors" from friends and supporters? Where do you stand on this issue? Write a brief statement that explains your judgments and the reasons behind them.

b. Thinking about your judgments:

- What values do you hold that support your judgment? What data, if any, support your judgment?

- What assumptions have you made about your position on this issue?

- What do you see as some potential consequences of the acceptance of "favors" for Supreme Court members?

- Should Supreme Court ethics be regulated by Congress? What is your judgment about this?

c. Extending your thinking:

- Despite the fact that there are no regulations about justices accepting favors, what should be the action, if any, of Congress to uphold Supreme Court ethics?

- How, in your judgment, is accepting favors by a Supreme Court justice different from or similar to accepting favors by a member of the House or Senate?

- What, if any, penalties should be given to justices accepting favors from donors and friends? What is your judgment about this?

- Justice Alito believes that the ethics of a Supreme Court member should be a matter of personal responsibility. What is your judgment about this?

2. Former president Donald Trump has now been indicted for several crimes regarding his involvement in the falsification of electoral college votes in the 2020 election, his removing secret and confidential files from his White House office to his home, and his deletion of consequential information from tapes essential to his prosecution. Despite these issues, he appears to be the leading candidate for the Republican nomination for president in the next (2024) election.

a. Should a person who is being charged with such crimes be given a chance to run for president? What is your judgment about this? Where do you stand on this issue? Write a brief statement that presents your judgment clearly.

b. Thinking about your judgment:

- What values do you hold that lie behind your judgment?

- What data, if any, support your judgment?

- Does the nature of the crimes for which Trump is being charged have anything to do with your judgment? In your thinking, is there a "scale" of offenses—the worst, the least bad—that informs your judgment?

- Is there a role you could play that will have any influence on others with the same or different judgments about this issue?

c. Extending your thinking:

- Suppose that despite the charges against him, Trump did win the Republican nomination. What values, in your view, might support the action of the nominating committee?

- Your neighbor says that "innocent until proven guilty" is the rule we should abide by with respect to the charges against Trump. Where do you stand on this issue? What judgment do you make about this issue?

- If Trump is convicted, is that sufficient to prevent him from running for the office of president? What is your judgment about this? Where do you stand on this issue?

3. J. Robert Oppenheimer, about whom a three-hour film has just been released, is considered by some as the brilliant scientist who is the "father of the atom bomb." He is also considered by others to be the agent of death, the person who unleashed a weapon that could, in effect, be the destruction of humankind.

   a. What judgment have you made about Oppenheimer? What values do you hold that support your judgment? Write a brief statement that explains your judgment and the reasons for your position.

   b. Thinking about your judgment:
      - Data are key in informing judgment. What data do you have about Oppenheimer that stand behind your judgment about him? How sound are the data? How do you know?
      - A person's values are also key in informing judgment. What values do you hold that support your judgment about Oppenheimer? From which sources do your values come? How secure are they in your mind?
      - Supporters of Oppenheimer claim that he played a significant role in bringing World War II to an end. Does such a claim influence your judgment? What data support your views?
      - Some supporters claim that Nazi Germany was also moving forward in their discovery of atomic power that would lead to the building of an atom bomb. And that is why Oppenheimer's role in being the first in that breakthrough

was so urgent. What is your position on this? Do these data in any way change your judgment?

c. Extending your thinking:

- More than a few of the scientists who participated in the Manhattan Project succumbed to cancer in the aftermath of their work with uranium. Some claim that this is their "just rewards" for unleashing such a weapon on civilization. What is your judgment about this? What values underlie that judgment? What data support it?

- It was President Harry Truman who decided to use the atom bomb on the Japanese cities of Hiroshima and Nagasaki, bringing a quick and destructive end to the Japanese role in World War II. In retrospect, claims have been made to suggest that the war was near an end anyway and that the destruction of these two cities was more a matter of revenge for the Japanese attack on Pearl Harbor. What is your judgment about the use of the bomb on these two cities? What values underlie that judgment? What data, if any, do you have that support your judgment?

4. A sitting president, Joe Biden, who will be 80 if and when he chooses to run for a second term, has been encouraged by some of his supporters to step down, citing his age as a factor that might impede his performance. After all, they claim, the president's job is one of the most difficult and challenging of all—and doing that strenuous, challenging, and overwhelming work may be over the top for an octogenarian. Can an 80-plus-year-old fulfill the functions of the presidency? Is his brain sufficiently active and "in gear" to tackle the various and complex problems of not only his country but also the world?

a. Where do you stand on the matter of age requirements for someone running for high office? What is your judgment about how age might influence their performance? What data do you have that support your judgment? Write a short statement that presents your judgment and the data that support it.

b. Thinking about your judgment:

- How would the nature of the role for which a candidate is running influence your judgment?
- Would your judgment be different if the office was for the Senate? A bus driver? A surgeon?
- What values do you hold that underlie your judgment about age and performance?
- What data do you have, so far, that impact on your judgment about age and performance?

c. Extending your thinking:

- What examples can you give of age discrimination? How does your judgment about age and performance relate to any of those examples?
- What other factors, besides age, might impact negatively on the performance of a candidate for high office? What examples can you give to support your ideas?
- What factors, besides age, might impact positively on the performance of a candidate for high office? What examples can you give to support your ideas?

CHAPTER 8

The Burdens of Living a Life of Reason

There's No Free Lunch

IT HAS ALREADY BEEN WRITTEN IN AN EARLIER CHAPTER THAT THERE are different ways of thinking. We think about the dinner menu, the best route from Newark to New York City during rush hour, the best ways to ensure that our children are safe and healthy, the best method to teach beginning reading, or the best pet to buy for apartment dwelling. We think about what we can do about climate change, about which savings plan is best for our retirement funds, about how to deal with a child's learning problems, or about how to help a person "of age" to find home care assistance.

Problem solving is an ongoing fact of life. Some of the problems we face require more rigorous and more challenging mental processing. They require more thoughtful application of several procedures that are examined and scrutinized to determine the effects. Some are more easily managed, less stressful, and less challenging, requiring less intellectual involvement.

In this book, an attempt has been made to promote awareness of those different types of intellectual functioning well as providing materials and activities that engage our higher-order mental skills. Should anyone undertake to participate in such a program to further their intellectual development? Should we be satisfied with being adept at the less complex forms of thinking that we routinely do as part of our daily activities?

In other words, why bother? What's the payoff for becoming more mature, more reasoned, more rational, and better equipped to take on the more formidable challenges that lie in wait for us?

Ah, as Hamlet said, "that is the question."

WHAT'S IMPORTANT?

During the past century, the peoples of the world have been witness to profound and extreme changes. Early in the 20th century, the automobile replaced the horse and wagon, bringing far-reaching changes not only on the roads but also in all manners of our lives. Reformers brought about new child labor laws, food safety laws, and increased rights for women and workers. Two world wars took countless lives and brought an end to imperialism and colonialism, dictatorships in Germany and Italy, and the spread of the Soviet empire into satellite countries.

Unprecedented advances in science and technology defined the latter part of the century. Oppenheimer's work at Los Alamos brought us into the Atomic Age—giving us the power to annihilate civilization with the touch of a button. Wars between nations have never ceased; tribes and splinter groups no longer need the support of a government to wreak havoc on their presumed enemies. Guns and weapons of mass destruction are accessed easily through more sources than we'd like to believe. And a human has walked on the moon.

A democratic government in the United States came under attack from an extreme right faction of a major political party. A former president has been indicted for crimes against the government. The moral codes of behavior on which we have previously depended seem eroded as political leadership bends to what is self-aggrandizing rather than what is true and good for the nation. The issues of human rights still form the mainframe of our national and international concerns.

A viral plague, as ruthless as the Spanish flu, put the world under attack and brought about quarantines, isolation, and fear of being among crowds. Conflicting data from different sources made us doubt the advice and warnings of our best medical practitioners. Political leaders used their bully pits to disparage and dismiss the advice of doctors. Who were we to believe?

Scientists rushed to develop a vaccine that would work to prevent illness, yet large groups of people took a strong stand against getting the vaccine and taking any precautions against infection. In the United States alone, more than 1 million people, thus unprotected, died from the virus. Organ transplants have become routine; a person can donate a living organ to someone in need of a kidney or heart.

Some climatologists warn that if we don't take extreme measures to combat the ruinous effects of toxins in the air we breathe and in the water we drink, we are in grave danger of risks to our health, increased drought, diminishing food supplies, and other serious and deadly consequences. The intense heat of summers and wildfires in some areas of the globe have sharpened concerns about the effects of climate change.

Technology has not only brought entertainment into our homes; the internet has given us access to immediate news and disinformation. More recently, artificial intelligence has been introduced into our lives—a system that can simulate human intelligence. Where do we go from here?

These are only a few of the issues that permeate our lives. They are only a fraction of what lies ahead. As change becomes more rapid and world problems become more intense, the question of how we act, how we choose, and how we address the problems that face us become more complex. How do we meet these challenges?

How do we provide ourselves with the tools to become more fully functioning members of our complex society in not only adapting to change but also helping us acquire insights into world problems and their solutions? The skills we have are useless unless they prepare us to meet problems that are new and that neither we nor anyone else have ever encountered before. The kind of thinking that asks us to make a choice about whether to have steak or fish for dinner will not suffice to deal with our uncertain future.

There are those who make a profession of being critical without contributing to any solutions. There are those who are frightened, disturbed, and even petulant. They want a return to some mythical times when the world was serene and hapless citizens were content with pat solutions to complex problems. And there are those who have the ability and the skills to look at what's ahead, to work together to find agreeable solutions, or, at the least, to find some ways to moderate and to improve what is on offer.

It is, of course, a matter of what's important to any individual reading this text: to be, or not to be; to improve one's own intelligent habits of mind, or to sit back and let others take the lead; to become more mature, more independent, and more skilled at dealing with complexities, or to pretend that it doesn't really matter; or to be content with complaining about the status quo, or to make one's own mark in helping to work for change for the better.

The "life of reason" is not one that can be put on like a new jacket. The bitter truth is that one has to work at improving those higher-order mental skills; the results accrue over time as one keeps working on the development of those intelligent habits of mind. No one can do it for you. The process brings to mind the response of the classical guitarist Andrés Segovia, who said to a student in his master's class, "The secret of my success is that I never practice my scales more than five hours a day."

This book has suggested a course of action for those who would embark on such a program of self-improvement—a program that would help to stretch minds, take cognitive risks, and be unafraid to face the new and complex problems that lie in the future. To develop such personal autonomy to think things through on one's own and to grow in one's ability to use one's cognitive powers to deal with the problems of the unknown with self-assurance and confidence—these are not skills that can be readily dismissed.

But there is more. There accrues, as a consequence of such development, a feeling of empowerment—that spirit of "can do" that can be attributed to an inner sense of competence to tackle a problem with confidence that you have the power to do this. In acquiring this sense of personal power, one feels pleasure and satisfaction, increased self-confidence, and heightened personal autonomy. There is a positive spirit about such people. When faced with a problem requiring some innovative procedures, they do not shirk but rather embrace the problem with positive energy. We trust them to find solutions, and their confidence in themselves fills us with confidence in them. When we see them in operation, taking charge and leading the way, we are full of admiration for them and for what they can do.

If thinking matters, then a course of action has been provided to enable those processes. No one said it was easy. But to put an emphasis on the improvement of the quality of thinking is to take a first long step toward an improvement of the human condition.

BIBLIOGRAPHY

Chase, Stuart. 1956. *Guides to Straight Thinking*. New York: Harper & Row.

Chotiner, Isaac. 2020. "Thomas Chatterton Williams on Race, Identity, and Cancel Culture." *The New Yorker*, July 22, https://www.newyorker.com/news/q-and-a/thomas-chatterton-williams-on-race-identity-and-cancel-culture.

Costa, Arthur. 1985. "The Behaviors of Intelligence." In *Developing Minds: A Resource Book for Teaching Thinking*, edited by Arthur L. Costa. Washington, DC: Association for Supervision and Curriculum Development.

Cummins, Eleanor, and Andrew Zaleski. 2023. "If Loneliness Is an Epidemic, How Do We Treat It?" *New York Times*, July 16, 6–7.

Davies, William. 2019. *Nervous States: Democracy and the Decline of Reason*. New York: Norton.

Feynman, Richard. 1985. *Surely, You're Joking, Mr. Feynman*. New York: Norton.

Ford, G. M. 2005. *No Man's Land*. New York: HarperCollins.

Garber, Megan. 2023. "We're Already in the Metaverse." *The Atlantic*, March, 18–27.

Hofstadter, Richard. 1963. *Anti-Intellectualism in American Life*. New York: Knopf.

Kahneman, Daniel. 2011. *Thinking Fast and Slow*. New York: Farrar, Straus and Giroux.

Morrell, David. 2013. *Murder as a Fine Art*. New York: Mulholland.

Paul, R., and I. Elder. 2002. *Critical Thinking: Tools for Taking Charge of Your Learning and Your Life*. Saddle River, NJ: Pearson.

Pogrow, Stanley. 2005. "HOTS Revisited: A Thinking Development Approach to Reducing the Learning Gap after Grade 3." *Phi Delta Kappan* 87, no. 1: 64–75.

Postman, Neil. 1985. *Amusing Ourselves to Death*. New York: Penguin.

Raths, Louis, E., Selma Wassermann, Arthur Jonas, and Arnold Rothstein. 1966. *Teaching for Thinking: Theory and Application*. Columbus, OH: Charles Merrill.

———. 1986. *Teaching for Thinking: Theory and Application*. New York: Teachers College Press.

Rokeach, Milton. 1960. *The Open and Closed Mind*. New York: Basic Books.

Rogers, Carl. 1961. *On Becoming a Person*. Boston: Houghton Mifflin.

Segal, Judith W., Susan F. Chipman, and Robert Glaser. 1985. *Thinking and Learning Skills*. Vols. 1 and 2. Hillsdale, NJ: Lawrence Erlbaum Associates.

Sternberg, Robert. 2007. *Teaching for Successful Intelligence*. Thousand Oaks, CA: Corwin.

Thompson, Robert. [1959] 1963. *The Psychology of Thinking*. London: Penguin.

Wassermann, Selma. 2009. *Teaching for Thinking Today*. New York: Teachers College Press.

———. 2020. *Evaluation without Tears*. Lanham, MD: Rowman & Littlefield.

Williams, Thomas Chatterton. 2023. "The French Are in a Panic over Le Wokisme." *The Atlantic*, March, 40–48.

ABOUT THE AUTHOR

Selma Wassermann is professor emerita in the Faculty of Education at Simon Fraser University and holder of the University Award for Teaching Excellence. She is the author of more than 30 books, including *The Play's the Thing: Promoting Intellectual and Emotional Development in the Early Childhood Years*, *Teaching Social Issues in the Middle Grades: A Teacher's Guide to Using Case Studies to Promote Intelligent Inquiry*, and *Teaching in the Age of Disinformation: Don't Confuse Me with the Data, My Mind Is Made Up*.

www.ingramcontent.com/pod-product-compliance
Lightning Source LLC
Chambersburg PA
CBHW030336270326
41926CB00010B/1647